The Importance
of
Being from Oshkosh

by

John Livingstone

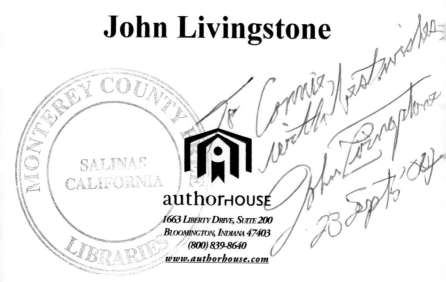

authorHOUSE

1663 LIBERTY DRIVE, SUITE 200
BLOOMINGTON, INDIANA 47403
(800) 839-8640
www.authorhouse.com

First published by AuthorHouse 06/28/04

ISBN: 1-4184-5509-1 (e)
ISBN: 1-4184-5508-3 (sc)

Library of Congress Control Number: 2004093230

Printed in the United States of America
Bloomington, Indiana

This book is printed on acid-free paper.

Acknowledgments

"You really ought to put that into a book." For many years friends have been offering me this advice.

But it took my *best friend's* (my wife's) suggestion, "You owe it to your children, grandchildren, and future great-grandchildren to put it down on paper."

I finally started jotting down little vignettes culled from memories of a fast-receding past. Suddenly, a book-sized manuscript became a reality.

So, first and foremost, I wish to thank my dear wife Nancy for her "positive vibes" about this project, and for her unremitting, though gentle encouragement.

My gratitude, too, goes to the fine Reference/Information Staff of the Oshkosh Public Library, a library of which any bigger city with greater resources would be proud. The biographical and historical information they furnished about Oshkosh's air pioneer Steve Wittman and Lumber Baron Nathan Paine, and the Paine Lumber Company helped me to separate myth from historical fact.

Thanks, also, to the Oshkosh Public Museum and its director Brad Larson, and to its long-ago director, Art Kannenberg, whose guided tours have inspired many hundreds of school children, including me to want to learn more about our hometown's colorful history. Although I didn't realize it at the time, it was Art Kannenberg who became a veritable mentor for me and many other children during the 'thirties.

Last, but by no means least, I wish to thank Kay Ambro of Carmel, California for her unstinting, courageous efforts to decipher my messy typing and convert it into something intelligible, readable, and I hope, entertaining.

John Livingstone
Carmel, California
June 2002

Introduction

The Importance of Being from Oshkosh is a collection of anecdotes and short essays by John Livingstone spanning the years of the Great Depression, the Second World War, and the Cold War as experienced by a son of the American middle-west, a youth who grew up swiftly.

As with many of his generation, John eagerly volunteered to serve in his country's armed forces, caught up in the fervor of wartime patriotism and hatred for the enemy, unmindful of what personal consequences might accrue. A barely subliminal desire to escape the doldrums of life in a depression-wracked small Wisconsin city, to be part of history in the making, made the world outside Oshkosh all the more enticing.

With education, time to reflect, and a maturity that living into the twenty-first century would provide, each of his glimpses into the fast-receding past might well be prefaced with "Now that I look back on it all..."

His has been a life as full of adventure, misadventure, humor, and pathos as anyone could ever wish for.

Table of Contents

*These chapters are adapted from the author's weekly column
"To Put It Mildly," published in the Monterey County Post.

1.

The Depression Years

The word "Oshkosh," to a Californian's ear, suggests toddlers' clothes and overalls, but the name of my hometown hasn't inspired the respect it deserves.

During World War II, my first contact with the world outside Oshkosh was when I enlisted in the army. The army sent me to an anti-aircraft artillery unit out on Long Island Sound to defend New York from German bombers. I was thrown in with a platoon of irrepressible Bronxites, Brooklynites and Manhattenites who had never before seen or even touched an Oshkoshite.

When it somehow came out that I was from Oshkosh, Wisconsin, they burst into gales of laughter. Why being from Oshkosh provoked such derision mystified me until my sergeant, an ex-math teacher from the Bronx, enlightened me.

"A New Yorker's mind has been twisted by countless stand-up comics' jokes about the 'sticks,' so to a New Yorker's ear, the sound of the word Oshkosh is synonymous with 'sticks'."

The passage of more than fifty years had almost completely erased a visceral reticence to reveal my roots until just recently. At a book-signing party, someone introduced me to a hyper-urbane snob pungently reminiscent of a reincarnated Oscar Wilde.

"And where might you be from?" He asked. (Such condescension! And he even ended his question in a preposition)!

I countered warily, "Oh, you probably have never heard of a town called Oshkosh; it's somewhere in the middle west."

"Of course I have. It's where overalls come from."

His attitude reminded me of a slur attributed to Montesquieu: "How could anyone possibly be Chinese?"

My adversary pressed on: "Tell me, Mr. -- what's your name? Is there anything about **that place** you miss?"

I parried the thrust. "Quite a lot, but it wouldn't merit mentioning in company such as this." I excused myself from his presence and retreated to the hors d'oeuvre table.

Despite the prosaic aura the name of my hometown seems to send forth, there are memories to savor, mostly about people and how much color and texture they added to a drab, depression-wracked town of 39,108 souls.

Early Recollections of the
Fair White City on the Winnebago Sea*

One of my earliest recollections of the "sticks" I hail from is when my parents, one autumn day in 1928 took me down to the Chicago & Northwestern train station in Oshkosh to say good-bye to the world-famous Wagnerian contralto, Madame Schumann-Heink. She had given a concert at Oshkosh's Grand Opera House (looking back on it now, "Grand" seems a bit pretentious). All the same, imagine: a "sticks" town of 39,108 souls having an opera house! And in the middle-west! As the diva stood at the railing of her Pullman car porch, she caught sight of my father in the crowd (he had helped arrange her visit). I was perched on his shoulders, dutifully obeying his order to blow a kiss in her direction. She beckoned to him to lift me up to her. As she pressed me to her generous bosom and kissed me on the forehead, the crowd cheered and applauded. Fearing an encore to that performance, I struggled to free myself from her heavily perfumed embrace. The strong aroma of her perfume made me gag, just as had happened a few days before when I stuck my nose into a jar of horseradish while at dinner at the Peacock Restaurant.

The train whistle hooted, and as the Pullman car lurched, Madame Schumann-Heink, eager to jettison me, looked for my father who had been blocked from her view by a tall policeman, Officer MacDonald. As the train slowly moved out of the station, it looked as if the great diva would have a three-year-old travelling companion. Officer MacDonald raced down the tracks, and shouted to her to drop me down to him. I landed in his arms like a medicine ball. Since that day the MacDonald family became close friends of ours.

~~~

*Title of a hundred-year-old Oshkosh guidebook.

2.

Sonic Recollections

Having been a professional photographer for over forty years, I would think my most vivid recollections about Oshkosh would be decidedly visual, rather than aural, but such is not the case. Except for a blackened heroic bronze bigger-than-life cluster of Union soldiers advancing on the rebels in Monument Square with the smoke-smudged old Grand Opera House forming a backdrop behind them, a Tudor-Gothic mansion built by lumber baron Nathan Paine during the depths of the Depression, and a pair of black bronze Trafalgar Square-look-a-like lions that graced the steps of our town's big-city-like Romanesque Public Library, my recollections have always been aural.

A factory town, Oshkosh had a quartet of factory whistles you could set your watch by. Every morning they summoned legions of lunch-pail toting workers to their daily grind; short, insistent blasts at noon proclaiming time off for lunch, then even longer, more insistent blasts calling the workers back to their work-benches and machines, as if impatient for their return. At five o'clock, long, mournful "quitting time" blasts revved up the activities of bartenders in Oshkosh's plentiful neighborhood taverns to get ready for an influx of tired, thirsty workers.

Every year, on Armistice Day, while we elementary school pupils stood squirming in our Rose C. Swart Training School auditorium, at precisely 11:00 a.m. all of our town's factory whistles commemorated the Fallen of the Great War to End All Wars for the longest two minutes imaginable. Our

4

music teacher, Miss Rose, while the whistles blew, would begin sobbing and dabbing her eyes with her handkerchief. Why we annually took such relish in seeing that sweet-natured little lady grieve over her fallen fiancée is something that defies explanation.

Two major rail lines cut through my town. The Soo Line skirted the back of the business district, its long rattling freight trains tying up Main Street-bound traffic while depositing yet another layer of soot on the east wall of the First Congregational Church. I had once seen a sooty church while visiting Chicago during the 1933 World's Fair, and I felt that my city was acquiring a big-city look, which filled me with pride.

The affluent east side of town was bisected by the Chicago & Northwestern Line. Its two sets of tracks, one going north and the other going south, had been laid by a British company, so naturally the north-bound tracks were on the left side and the south-bound tracks were on the left side, never to become Americanized, as far as I can tell. The sudden, staccato blasts from its locomotives shook crockery in houses along the tracks, but saved many a car from demolition at grade crossings.

On hot summer nights, when the thermometer might mercifully come down to eighty degrees, Oshkoshers, who would abandon their hot second story bedrooms in favor of a mattress on the living room floor downstairs or on the front porch, could listen all night to the mournful distant dirge of train whistles that pierced the night air outside of town, and the buzz of millions of lake flies against the porch screens, a bane for light sleepers.

During my last summer in Oshkosh, in 1946, my tastes in music took a definite downturn when I fell into the

5

habit of frequenting a roadhouse at the north end of town, Lou Klimko's Club 41. The club's main draw was its dance band, a noisy, spirited combo led by a saxophone-wielding, piano thumping musical celebrity, Joe Wiseapple. The name he endured was probably an Anglicized version of the German name Weissapfel. His swing and jazz numbers were brassy, loud, easy to dance to. Club 41 was The Place to meet off-duty nurses, telephone operators and seamstresses from the Oshkosh B'Gosh Overall factory. Strong competitors for the affections of Oshkosh music lovers were three or four polka bands that held sway at roadhouses south of town, attracting mainly farm boys, house maids and blue-collar workers every Saturday night.

When I was about five, perched on my grandfather's thirty-second degree Masonic shoulders, I witnessed a parade of white plume-hatted knights of some sort and a procession of fez-topped Shriners led by a Shriner's band playing an oriental-sounding, minor key melody that I can still recall, note for note, to this day. Why this of all melodies should have stuck with me for over seventy years has me completely baffled. Among my more far-out theories is that in a previous incarnation I may have heard it or played it many times, or even may have written it. Some sixty years after having heard it at that Masonic parade, when I chanced to hear it again, I asked a musician friend if he had ever heard it before. He replied rather inexactly that it was some kind of Turkish march.

In March, 1963 I revisited Oshkosh, and experienced what could be described as a strong feeling not of *déjà vue* but of *déjà écouté*. The sounds of tire chains and coal sliding down chutes into the basements of houses, muffled by the snow drifts, sounds I hadn't heard for more than forty years in my part of California, - all came back as familiar to me as if I had heard them yesterday.

The sounds of my old hometown are humble, prosaic sounds, not unique, I'm sure, to just one middle-western town; nonetheless, they are for me sounds never to be forgotten, always to be savored, for they are hometown sounds of a bygone era.

~~~

3.

Teachers and Twins

Miss Scott, my eighth grade teacher, was a long, affable, lanky lady with a decidedly un-Oshkosh way of speaking. It was a slight, though inescapable drawl that I was to realize many years later was typical of farmers from southern Indiana or southern Illinois.

She was a living, breathing, talking image of Grant Wood's *American Gothic* farmer's wife, not as stern, but with her greying hair swept severely back in a bun, and her just plain down-on-the farm looks. Miss Scott usually wore a long, faded blue print dress with little green flowers on it; whether it be winter, spring or fall, it made no difference. It was her favorite dress, complete with a matching slender cloth belt that hung limply over her narrow hips.

What impressed me and my classmates about our teacher was not so much how she pronounced what she taught us, but her inevitable, day-in and day-out theme: "Now boys and girls, never forget how all-important it is for you, each and every one of you, to be a *Good Citizen*, not only just for your own sake, but for your family's, your community's and your nation's sake."

To this day, whenever I see a candy wrapper or a cigarette butt tossed on the sidewalk, there comes to mind Miss Scott's cheerful admonition, "Above all, be a Good Citizen!" Just a few days ago, while shopping at a supermarket, I absentmindedly placed back on a shelf a box of cereal I decided not to buy. After several yards down the aisle, it came to me that I had placed it on a shelf where it didn't belong. (I'm not being a Good Citizen), I thought, and felt impelled to hurry back to the scene of my near-misdemeanor and put the box where it belonged. Such was the lasting power of Miss Scott's teaching. I'm sure that not only I, but perhaps many dozens of former Oshkoshers, no matter what their station in life or location, were bound to be *Good Citizens* most of the time, if not all of the time.

Recently I witnessed a driver downtown in Carmel erasing a meter-maid's chalk mark from his tire. A question arose: should I be a *Good Citizen* and report this nefarious act to the police? I saw in my mind's eye Miss Scott nodding and smiling affirmatively. Upon reflection, however, it occurred to me that we are now living in a different era, a highly litigious one, and I decided that being a *Good Citizen* wouldn't be worth the risk of enduring what happens to "whistle blowers" in our society.

If Miss Scott were here today, she would have to concede that we are living in different times. I hope she would not judge me too harshly.

It Takes One to Know One

Speaking of regional accents, a few years ago while I was visiting an elementary school in King City, California, my keen ear for the spoken vowels and consonants of my fellow Americans earned me a brisk rebuff. As I approached the principal's office a youngster dashed past me, running at full speed down the empty corridor, evidently late for a class. A teacher happened just then to emerge from the principal's office and bent on enforcing the school's sacrosanct "No Running in the Halls" edict, shouted at the boy, "Yoo stahp ryte theyre!" (You stop right there!). Those four, emphatic words gave me a start. It wasn't what she said, but how she pronounced those vowels! They couldn't have come from anywhere in the world than my old hometown, Oshkosh, Wisconsin. I would have bet my life on that!

I couldn't resist rushing up to the teacher and blurting out,

"Pardon me, Miss, but you're from Oshkosh, aren't you?"

The teacher glowered at me as if I had hurled some unwarranted insult at her.

"Hell, no! I'm from Fahn doo lac!" (Fond du Lac), she retorted.

Whoops! I had missed my linguistic target by some seventeen or eighteen miles! That I had placed that unfortunate woman from Oshkosh was more than she could graciously accept. It then occurred to me that Little Fond du Lac, half the size of Oshkosh, was always a bit envious of its Big Brother to the North, my fair white city on the Winnebago Sea. Besides, hadn't Fond du Lac lost far more of its sons than Oshkosh during World War One?

So much for hazarding a guess as to one's linguistic roots, even though I think I'm good at it. The next time I hear someone who sounds like a Gangbusters character, or a Big Apple racketeer, I'm not breathing a word to him about his tell-tale speech patterns. It could be hazardous to my health.

"Paint Pot" and "Flour Barrel"

A familiar sight during the 1930's along Washington Boulevard (yes, the "sticks" even have boulevards) was a pair of elegantly dressed twin sisters. It was next to impossible to ascertain their age; one was coated with thick layers of face cream, and the other wore so much face powder and rouge you could only hazard a guess that they were over sixty and under ninety. Nobody seemed to know their names. They were usually referred to as "Paint Pot" and "Flour Barrel".

Daily, as if by clockwork, they would routinely walk down to the Chicago & Northwestern train depot to meet the 4:10 train out of Chicago. Neither rain nor sleet nor snow deterred them from their daily pilgrimage to the depot. It was commonly thought that they were infatuated with the locomotive engineer, – or was it the locomotive? It was hard to tell. They would stand in awe of either the iron horse or its driver, who would wait until the train was about to leave the depot to poke his head out of his cab and wave back at them.

In Oshkosh, where eccentricity was not encouraged or applauded, there must have been a lot of ungratified curiosity about two such colorful and enigmatic characters. Their anonymity, all things considered, seems to have remained intact.

Mademoiselle from Armentières

Oshkosh could boast of having a genuine, native-born French teacher, Mlle Mercier. She had been gravely wounded during the first World War. Her head and facial scars were to some extent concealed by her wearing a coal-black wig with long, straight sides and thick bangs across her forehead. She always seemed to me to have lived a lonely, isolated life, her only satisfaction derived from teaching us provincials a thing or two about French civilization, and its great contribution to culture, its literature. Not many towns during those depression years were fortunate enough to provide instruction in French free of an American accent, but Oshkosh was. As far as the teaching Spanish was concerned, that was quite another story.

My Spanish Teacher,
Señorita Kleinschmidt

In 1937 my parents sponsored immigration of a married couple, refugees from the Spanish civil war. Maria worked as a maid (three dollars a week, plus room and board), and Raimundo kept up the yard and garden, for which he, too, was paid handsomely. My father got him a job teaching Spanish to adults at the local teacher's college's night school. I had already had a couple of semesters of Latin, and for some strange, inexplicable reason, I enjoyed learning such a complicated, utterly foreign language. So, when my parents suggested I attend Raimundo's night classes, they must have been pleasantly surprised when I didn't put up any fight, but accepted their suggestion peaceably. Raimundo's Spanish class consisted of about ten adults, mostly late middle-aged or worse. I was, to my surprise, far brighter than the whole class put together when it came to memorizing long lists of Spanish vocabulary. My knowledge of Latin was a tremendous advantage over my fellow students, and I never missed an opportunity to remind them by pointing out to my instructor, for all to hear, that the Spanish word he just added to our vocabulary list was derived from the Latin *so-and-so*. Now that I look back on it, I should have realized that I was shunned socially after each class not because of my twelve years of age, but due to my enervating precocity.

Teachers and Twins

By the year 1940, my continual contact with the Spanish language with Raimundo as my mentor and instructor had created a monster, as far as my high school Spanish teacher, Señorita Kleinschmidt, was concerned. Her sole qualification to teach Spanish was having passed an intensive ten-week summer course in Spanish at La Escuela del Verano, in Mexico City. By my standards, not only was her knowledge of Spanish grammar and vocabulary rudimentary, to say the most, but her pronunciation, atrociously German-American, could never hold a candle to my, by that time, practically flawless Castilian.

Being totally committed to protecting my fellow students from her misinformation and her total lack of respect for the sound of the language, I missed few opportunities to call her down in class and to correct her, hoping that thereby the whole class would benefit. My earnest efforts on behalf of my classmates had a decided boomerang effect. Not only did Señorita Kleinschmidt treat me as an invisible non-entity, but she created a degrading daily duty for me to perform after class: cleaning the blackboards and erasers, and sweeping the floor. Worse, still, my efforts on behalf of my fellow students went unappreciated, even resented by them.

When on one final occasion, I challenged my Mexican-speaking teacher on the true meaning of the word *ganga*, I insisted that it meant *bargain*, and not *gang*. My tormentee, in a rage, grabbed a ruler and raised it threateningly over my head. Only her Teutonic self-control prevented the ruler from carrying out her original intention.

I sensed that sooner or later, I was bound to receive a blow, so I told my parents that I was afraid of being attacked by Señorita Kleinschmidt. My father, suspecting that I had provided ample provocation, tended to side with my teacher.

My mother, on the other hand, maintained that no amount of provocation justified a teacher to strike a fourteen-year-old child, no matter how obnoxious, to which I agreed wholeheartedly.

It was decided that some sort of "truce" be arranged between my teacher and me. My parents sent her a written invitation to come to our home to "discuss the matter". I was surprised when I was told she had accepted. In the meantime, I was to pretend nothing had happened, and to refrain from any further attempts to educate my teacher or to save my class from her repertoire of misinformation.

On the day before the appointed interview, I was given the chore of washing all the windows of our living room (our maid didn't "do windows"). I was ordered to stay out of the room during the interview, which I interpreted to mean that I could eavesdrop on the discussion from the next room.

Señorita Kleinschmidt arrived right on time, bearing a little potted plant for my mother, which was unsettling to me. My mother, by previous agreement with my father, did all the talking. After initial pleasantries were exchanged, my mother launched her "discussion" with: "I understand you have been teaching for only three years."

"Yes, that's true. During those three years I have been able to deal successfully with many difficult children, but I must admit that your son has me baffled as to how to deal with him. As you know, he's very bright, and eager to learn, but he is still an immature child. He confuses his place in the class as a student, not as a teacher. Since he is so advanced in Spanish, I would like to suggest that he be given credit for having passed the entire year with a grade of "A", and that he use that available class time to improve his homework assignments in math, social studies, biology and Latin."

(She's full of revenge), I thought, (and my mother is going to give in).

My mother was taken aback at the teacher's own assessment of the problem I was causing in her class. My teacher was that eager to get rid of me that she would even give me all "A's" for the course if only I would leave.

I had never enjoyed the least amount of popularity among my fellow students, (I invariably received the least number of valentines in our home-room valentine box), and I had always attributed it to the fact that I was the smallest boy in the class, the most likely perennial candidate for being trounced and bullied. It hadn't yet dawned on me that I was using my relatively high I.Q as a compensation for my low self-esteem, that I was overly eager to impress my peers and teachers with the only thing I really shined in, my knowledge of Spanish. I was not feeling sorry for my tormented, embattled teacher, not having cared about what a thorn I had become in her side, until that day when she nervously faced my parents.

A compromise was reached, and I was allowed to remain in her class if I would be respectful and considerate of her, and not ever contradict her again. And of course, my janitorial duties were ended. Best of all, I was saved from having to do extra homework. My parents remarked that Señorita Kleinschmidt looked worn and haggard. They suspected I had contributed to her run-down condition, of that I'm sure.

A year later an article appeared on the local newspaper's obituary page, announcing the death of Miss Carole Kleinschmidt, due to a long bout with cancer.

~~~

4.

The Raulf, a Sheik and a Lineman

A tall, handsome new hotel punctuated Oshkosh's flat skyline during the nineteen thirties. Named after its owner, Conrad Raulf, the Raulf Hotel incorporated in its high ceilinged lobby an exotic Gardens of the Alhambra décor complete with a rather annoying fountain, which, Mr. Raulf, an elderly gentleman, soon had turned off. In the basement of his hotel he grandly included a bowling alley and a miniature golf course. When he discovered that the miniature golf course was drawing patrons away from the more profitable bowling alley, he closed it forever. At the very top of his ten-story edifice he installed a stout, extra-tall flagpole, eminently suited for hosting a series of itinerant flagpole sitters. You could phone them at any hour and answer their questions about how you were doing in school, or what you wanted to be when you grew up, or you could ask them how they went to the bathroom up there on the flagpole. My parents took me downtown to watch these daredevils through a pair of mother-of-pearl covered opera glasses.

On the Raulf's second floor was a large ballroom with mirrored walls and sconces to add a touch of elegance and sophistication to any wedding reception or coming-out party. Every Thursday afternoon and night the ballroom became the site of the Raulf's weekly "Walkathon". This offered some twenty or thirty housemaids on their weekly afternoon and evening off a much looked forward-to chance to meet some thirty or forty unemployed young men and to walk around the dance floor until either their feet went numb or they dropped from exhaustion; all this for the then substantial sum of twenty-five cents a head. The Walkathon also drew Civilian Conservation Corps youths on leave from nearby C.C.C. camps, sporting their rough olive drab army uniforms. Laura, our maid, regularly felt drawn to these green-shirted would-be casanovas, only to find that their attentions and intentions were not always honorable. They invariably seemed to expect something more than a "thank you" for escorting her home at one in the morning.

Laura, a farm girl from the north woods of Wisconsin, accompanied my family to Chicago to attend the World's Fair in 1933, and my mother had to warn her repeatedly about gaping open-mouthed at the skyscrapers while pigeons flew overhead. Laura's favorite form of recreation after the Walkathon was to listen to radio station WLS, the Prairie Farmer Station out of Chicago, sending into her little bedroom the National Barn Dance program on Saturday nights. She learned to play a few cords on a guitar, and tearfully sang her favorite hillbilly song, the words of which still echo in my brain:

> *"Oh they cut down the ol' pine tree*
> *an' they hauled it away to the mill,*
> *to make a coffin of pine*
> *for that sweetheart of mine,*
> *Oh they cut down the ol' pine tree."*

The Raulf Hotel's barbershop held a special attraction for some of the town's ladies: a tall, olive-complected barber with patent leather-looking hair beguiled them with his Rudolph Valentino looks and smoldering personality. Mothers, who ordinarily would drop off their sons for haircuts at other barbershops, were inclined to accompany them and even forsake their beauty shop appointments to have "the Sheik" do their hair. When on occasion there weren't any mothers present, "the Sheik" would lecture us boys at length on the subject of sexual attraction between girls and boys, that it was a God-given gift, nothing to be ashamed of, that when young people experimented with sex, they were like "little birds, ready to try their wings, to leave the nest." Another topic he was fond of discoursing on was the horrors of trench warfare which he had experienced in France during the Great War. To us young boys his accounts of what befell him fifteen years before were pure ancient history.

Another barber, who had a shop farther up on Main Street was also a veteran of the Great War, but he happened to have been on the losing side. Jake the Barber, from Dusseldorf, one of the town's more outspoken Nazis, once gave me so much food for thought that when I brought it home to share with my parents, I was ordered never to step foot in his shop again.

Who in Oshkosh of the 'thirties could ever forget Charlie Clark, the singing lineman? The telephone company lineman was blessed with good looks and a pleasing though untrained operatic voice. From high up on telephone poles, Charlie enjoyed singing to admiring, culturally deprived housewives. Gossip had it that the gregarious "singing lineman" often accepted invitations to "come down and have a cup of coffee." There were those who insisted that he got somewhat less tangible rewards from some of his adoring fans. His defenders and apologists asserted that it was a mere coincidence that the neighborhoods in which he worked had a higher birth rate than the other neighborhoods. But then, as now, gossip is small town stuff. In New York one would never pass on such theoretical conjectures, would one?

~~~

5.

My Fundamentalist and Episcopal Pals

During my elementary school years my best friend was a fellow classmate, Stanley Anderson. He had big ears and a good heart. Though he towered over me, he always showed me respect and trust, something that eluded me as far as most of my fellow students were concerned. He was the son of a fundamentalist preacher, which may have contributed to his being, to my way of thinking, overly truthful, cautious and virtuous. But we did have one thing in common: our shared distress at having to take violin lessons from a Prussian-type bully, who was a better car salesman than a violin teacher. More about Stanley later. I only mention him now to make a rather inconsequential, though intriguing point: during my teen years I befriended yet another son of a man of the cloth, Richard Otto. He came from a well-to-do family that lived in a fine house on Oshkosh's elegant Algoma Boulevard. His father was Vicar of the town's Episcopal Church. Judging by the elegance of the cars that were parked out in front of the church every Sunday, his father, or his religion must have been doing an awful lot of things right, I figured - But then, of course, one could deduce the same thing when passing by the dignified edifice of the First Church of Christ Scientist, where my parents attended, adding their gleaming new car to the impressive collection of luxury cars parked in front of that church.

What I admired about Richard was his devil-may-care attitude, and especially the fact that he had a beautiful, refined sister, Jacquiline. When Richard was seventeen, he was the proud possessor of a driver's license, and a four-door 1920's vintage Hudson Super-six convertible with firm red leather seats that went up high in the back of the car. He was never able to get the side windows up, but that didn't prevent us from piling into his old open car, rain or shine, blizzard or sleet, crossing a farmer's field to pick up one kid who lived outside the city limits, and delivering us, almost always on time, to school. I had a special reason for looking forward to that daily, hectic ride to school: I often ended up sitting in that high-backed leather seat jammed in next to his sister, Jacquiline. It was during those frequent occasions that I derived the most pleasure imaginable from the physical principle of centrifugal force. On one most memorable occasion, as Richard took a particularly sudden turn to the right, I remarked to Jacquiline, "Isn't centrifugal force wonderful?" She pretended not to hear me.

Richard and his father, I gathered, didn't see eye to eye on many things. He would grumble to me about his father's lofty "holier than thou" attitude, and that despite his father's obvious wealth, he made Richard earn his weekly allowance by "piling on" chores, the most irksome being to climb up into his church's carillon tower, to play hymns at vesper time every evening that could be heard all over the city of Oshkosh. I often accompanied Richard up into the tower, and marvelled at his dexterity in handling the big wooden levers which struck the bells at just the right tempo.

One evening, Richard, in a particularly petulant mood, 'phoned me and asked me if I would like to hear something "special" that he would play on the chimes that evening. I sensed that he was troubled about something, so I agreed to go with him in his car to the church. During an uncharacteristically slow ride down to the church, Richard didn't say a word. Once we got up into the tower, he said, "Jack, brace yourself!"

The thought came to me that he was about to do something desperate, maybe even to jump out of the tower. To my immense relief, he placed a sheet of music on the stand, and began to apply an unusual amount of force and vigor to the levers. He seemed to be venting his anger on the levers. That was no typical hymn he was now playing, not by a long shot. What he had chosen was a most inappropriate piece of music ever to come out of a church tower, *The Beer Barrel Polka*. It was heard all over the beer-loving city of Oshkosh. I would have tried to intervene had I not been four inches shorter and twenty pounds lighter than Richard. But I also figured that when he returned home that night, there certainly would be hell to pay.

Soon afterward, Richard enlisted in the Army Air Corps.

~~~

6.

Crime in the 'Thirties

There's a lot of concern these days about juvenile crime. When I was growing up in Oshkosh, "juvenile crime" had a long way to go before it would become a household word. The closest thing to "crimes" committed by children and adolescents then was an occasional shop-lifting or an overly destructive Halloween prank. I recall as if it were yesterday when at the age of five or six, I wandered away from my parents in the local Sears & Roebuck store down on lower Main Street, long enough to pocket a yellow folding yardstick with black numbers on it, which I coveted so much I couldn't stand to leave the store without it. The torment that followed, the worry about having it discovered once I got home far outweighed its intrinsic value, which in 1930 would have amounted to about twenty-five cents. My parents, stern disciplinarians, would have taken me down to the store manager and I would have had to admit my guilt, apologize and promise never to do such an awful thing ever again. My ill-gotten yardstick soon ended up buried two feet down in a hole I had begun in our back yard, a hole I had been assured would reach China if I kept on digging long enough. Seventy years later, I may forget where I park my car in downtown Carmel, but I'm certain I could find immediately my buried booty at 177 Central Avenue, if I ever got back to Oshkosh.

There was the occasional school yard criminal type, a bully, a living testimonial to the Darwinian thesis of survival of the fittest. He was always bigger and stronger than his intended victims. He got his enjoyment out of life by intimidating and terrorizing smaller, weaker kids such as myself. Every once in awhile a smaller but tougher kid would stand up to him, and his budding criminal career would be put on hold.

Speaking of budding criminal types, there was one among the crowd that hung out at Schroeder's Drugstore, on Jackson Drive, *R.N.* One day, I was riding my bike home from school, and as I was approaching the Jackson Drive intersection at high speed, I applied my brakes to slow down as a horse-drawn Carver Dairy milk wagon loomed in front of me. My brakes failed completely. As I sailed through the intersection I had to jump off the bike and drag my feet along the pavement to bring it to a stop. It was then that I found that each of my bike's two brake cables had been disconnected. It occurred to me that this might be the work of someone who disliked me. That could have been any number of kids whose dad had an older car than my dad had, or whose mother wore plainer dresses and hats than my mother did. But there was one kid who was mean enough and stupid enough to carry out such a crime, R.N. I'm not mentioning his name lest he still be around and now is living an upright, law-abiding life, admired by his children and grandchildren, and possibly even by his wife. It was R.N. who never hesitated to show his resentment and envy of me. My cardinal sin in his eyes was that I had a newer, better Schwinn racing bike than he had or would ever hope to have. It bothered him to watch me spend a major portion of my weekly allowance at Schroeder Drugstore soda fountain on fifteen-cent malted milks or a couple of Cokes laced with chocolate syrup at five cents each. Whenever I sat at the soda fountain he would try to stare me down. If it hadn't been for big Bob Schroeder's presence behind the counter, he would have tried to take me out in back of the store for a one-sided tussle. But Bob, the son of the owner, was my best and most reliable protector. He was big and muscular, and in his twenties, and despite the difference in our ages, he seemed to enjoy having us kids hanging around his store, even if it meant that we showed little respect for the hot-off-the-press condition of his racks of comic books and magazines, many of which became so dog-eared that they were no longer saleable, especially the *Sunshine and Health* nudist magazines. Some of our number acquired the habit of skipping school and used his store as a refuge from the truant officer. When Bob spotted the truant officer approaching the store, he would hustle the truants down into his coal cellar until the man left.

Bob was aware of the constantly shifting system of alliances and cliques among his young customers, and that he held undisputed balance of power over those sometime antagonistic groups. We all knew for certain that to make Bob angry meant banishment from his store.

A day after my near-extinction at the hands of R.N. I decided to confront my would-be assassin in Bob's presence, accuse him of the crime, and let the chips fall where they may. In order to impress Bob, and to make an impression on R.N. the seriousness of his offense, I took a discarded popsicle stick and a short length of piano wire, constructed a medically-impressive-looking splint, bound it with surgical tape with a piano wire loop extending beyond my "broken" fingertip to provide a protective bumper. I arrived at the soda fountain with my finger trussed up like a mummy. Pointing to my "broken" finger, I said, "Bob, because of R.N., I had a nearly fatal accident yesterday. My brake cables were disconnected and I could have been killed at this intersection." R.N., who was nearby, sneered and said, "You gotta watch them brake cables. They break real easy."

He then turned around to what he expected to be a supportive, appreciative audience. Bob, infuriated, shook his big fist in R.N.'s face and shouted, "Get out of my store and don't show your face around here again!"

There was a downside of this episode. I had to remove the "splint" each time I arrived home, and put it on again each day before arriving at school or the drugstore, a charade which would last two long weeks.

~~~

7.

A Farewell to Strings

It's a long way from Oshkosh High School Auditorium to New York's Carnegie Hall, I was to find out eventually.

My career as a concert violinist began in 1937. My hometown, NRA sign-besotted, groggy, slumbering, had been hit hard by the Great Depression. Hundreds of unemployed workers drove in their model A Fords to City Hall to pick up their relief checks. At the same time, Oshkosh was experiencing a cultural renaissance, thanks to the Federally funded Works Progress Administration, which was breathing new life into despondent artists, musicians and thespians by providing them with places to practice their art with subsistence incomes.

Not far from my house the WPA had taken over a run-down old mansion, creating a "social club" atmosphere for out-of-work men. The main living room became the Card Room, where King Cribbage reigned supreme. Upstairs a tiny British Septuagenarian, Mr. Ryder, replete with pince-nez glasses, gave free instruction in foil, épée and sabre fencing to teenaged boys. I was never told that economic status would rule out my being admitted to Mr. Ryder's classes, but noticing the poverty level of the clothes of his students, I left nothing to chance. I would race home after school, put on my oldest, shabbiest clothes, and return to the WPA Clubhouse, determined to blend in.

Under Mr. Ryder's tutelage I acquired a trait that otherwise would have eluded me: assertiveness. His oft-repeated dictum of attack, parry, riposte (counterattack) made an indelible impression on a heretofore passive, defenseless kid. I never became an expert fencer, but the sport inculcates in everyone who takes it up a positive attitude toward winning, of defending oneself "con brio" (with verve), as my teacher was fond of repeating. To this day, Mr. Ryder's fencing instruction has enabled me to hold my own in arguments and altercations by a strategy of attack, defense, feints and counter-attack, no matter how specious or fallacious my position may seem to the opposition.

Coming home one night from a violin concert at Oshkosh's old Grand Opera House, my parents heard me whistling my version of the performer's rendition of a Paganini variation. My father was so impressed, he peremptorily decided that I would become a world-famous violinist. All of my Ryderesque defensive tactics came to naught in the face of overwhelming parental coercion, backed by such irrefutable logic as "You owe it to us and to your country to make a name for yourself", and "You may be weak in arithmetic, science, Latin and penmanship, but that's no reason why you can't be brilliant in music." No amount of Mr. Ryder's indoctrination could have stymied this mode of attack. I surrendered, grudgingly agreeing to take violin lessons.

My parents engaged one of the two violin teachers extant in Oshkosh at the time, a Mr. Edward Gumbacher. The other teacher, Mr. Laffee, advertised his Masonic connections by requiring his child students to wear a Shriner's fez when they posed for a group advertisement photo. This did not sit well with my father, possibly because he had once suffered the humiliation of having been black-balled by the Benevolent Protective Order of the Elks.

Mr. Gumbacher sold cars during the day at the local Chrysler-Plymouth-DeSoto agency, and taught violin in the evenings. His fee was astronomical: *two dollars* an hour, a sacrifice I hoped my parents would find too much to bear, *sooner*, rather than later. Good salesman that he was, on his initial visit to our house he brought along his violin and treated my parents to a cloying rendition of Fritz Kreisler's *Liebesleid* (Love's Lament). I preferred to think that the tears in my mothers eyes were due to his high fee, and not to *Liebesleid*. My parents were completely sold, even to the extent of grasping a "once in a lifetime" opportunity to pay the numbing sum of fifty dollars for a resin-coated Irish violin inlaid with mother of pearl shamrocks for their embryonic violin virtuoso. To this day I suspect that the shamrocks, contrary to Mr. Gumbacher's hints, did absolutely nothing to improve the tone of the instrument. It's tonal quality would be entirely up to me, in the distant future, if ever.

My first lesson took place at my teacher's house. A snarling German Shepherd named Otto von Bismarck met me at the door. Once safely inside, I was ceremoniously handed the Irish violin and bow. I instinctively grasped the bow with my left hand, a natural reaction for a southpaw, to the horror of Mr. Gumbacher. Having grown up in a predominantly German community, I knew German when I heard it. The torrent of German swear words and invectives was topped off by a word I was to hear frequently over the ensuing years, *"Dumkopf!"*

If that first lesson was any indication, my road to mastery of the violin was to be a long, flat one, filled with pot holes.

As soon as I returned home, I complained about my rough treatment at the hands of Mr. Gumbacher and Otto von Bismarck, hoping this would put an end to my career before it even started. But my parents, more than ever resolute to realize something out of their heavy initial investment, wouldn't budge, except to compromise by having my teacher come to our house to give me my weekly lesson in their presence.

So it came to pass that every Wednesday evening, at supper-time, Mr. Gumbacher would arrive while I was finishing my supper, seated in front of the radio in the living room, listening to the closing commercial and theme song of "Jack Armstrong, All-American Boy". My teacher would join my parents at the dining-room table, having dessert with them while I sawed away at my bowing studies (pronounced by my teacher as *"eetoods,"* which years later I learned to pronounce the proper French way, *"études"*).

Between mouthfuls of apple strudel my teacher urged me on, reassuring his by now somewhat dubious patrons that their son was "full of promise, of hidden talent, just waiting to be tapped."

After a year of "tapping", Mr. Gumbacher announced to my parents that the time would soon come for me to make my first public performance, at his annual recital. Each of his students was to play one selection. The recital was a couple of months off, so he began the tedious job of teaching me to play a jerky, vibratoless *Humoresque*. After many hours of honing and polishing, that rough gem began to take shape. As the weeks wore on, my parents began to notice a definite improvement, and they were looking forward to that big day as much as I was dreading it. As she listened to my incessant practicing of *Humoresque*, Mother would sigh and say softly, "My son, the violinist is on his way."

My best friend, Stanley Anderson, the son of a hell-fire and brimstone preacher, was also one of Mr. Gumbacher's pupils. One afternoon after school, we were practicing at Stanley's house *La Golondrina* as a duet. His father, sprawled on the living room floor, was preparing a chart showing the transmigration of souls. He was busily coloring in sketches of grasshoppers, ants, elephants and monkeys, while we were producing what approximated the sound of a melody. He snapped his finger at us and announced,

"Boys, that's it! Keep practicing that song, and I'll have you play it to the congregation some Sunday."

I was inclined to interpret this more as a threat than a promise. My hopes evaporated a few nights later when the Reverend Anderson, on the 'phone, forged a commitment with my parents for me to appear *in concert* with Stanley at the Oshkosh Gospel Tabernacle the following Sunday. My parents, although sometime Christian Scientists, saw no reason why they and I should not set foot in an extremely fundamentalist church, since their son, the violinist was to make his public debut.

So excited were they about my first public appearance, they took me to the Continental, an upscale clothing store on Main Street. They bought me the most elegant pair of blue gabardine pants I'd ever seen, then or since. Mother, glancing at the price tag, blanched at the thought of parting with five dollars for a pair of kid's pants, but my father, in an ebullient mood, calmed her by reassuring her, "Our son not only has got to *sound* good, but *look* good, too."

I was thrilled with my new blue gabardine pants. The thought came to me, (*if one "la Golondrina" can do this for me, what will one "Humoresque" next month do for me?*)

It was a cold winter day when we arrived at the little wooden Oshkosh Gospel Tabernacle. We sat bundled up in our coats in the unheated church through a lengthy, firey sermon interspersed by several exuberantly delivered hymns by the small congregation, led by an emaciated trombonist. Then the Great Moment arrived. Stanley and I marched up the aisle, our violins couched under our elbows, and our bows swinging as we marched. Shaking from nerves as well as the cold, we set up our music stands, turned to *La Golondrina*, carefully set the metal page keepers in place, and launched into our much-practiced performance. We were playing well, at least we thought so, and exchanged reassuring glances away from the page. At the conclusion of our offering, we bowed to the audience. There was no applause, no standing ovation, no shouts of "Encore" as we packed up our music stands and went back to our pews.

On the way home, my mother told me, "You don't get applauded in a church, silly! Did the preacher or the trombone player get any applause? Of course, not!"

My father, all smiles, said, "You did well, real well! Even Abraham Lincoln got no applause after his Gettysburg Address."

I had a hard time equating a speech by Abraham Lincoln with my playing of *La Golondrina*, but I never made an issue of it.

By the end of my first year, I was considered well enough advanced to replace the first violinist (who hoped Mr. Laffee might be a better teacher) in the Gumbacher Symphony Choir (which contained ten violinists, a viola player and a cellist, but not one singer). This annual event was Mr. Gumbacher's supreme public relations effort to convince our music-loving community that he could make silk purses out of sows' ears.

The concert was held in Oshkosh High School's old run-down auditorium. My parents were chagrined and grumbled about the fact that it should have taken place in the Grand Opera House (equally run-down), a more appropriate setting, with better acoustics, they thought. Parents, neighbors, relatives and teachers filled the hall. The first selection, lamentably, was the Star Spangled Banner. Mr. Gumbacher had intended to start off the concert with a bang, stirring the emotions of the audience with a patriotic piece. But we stumbled through it badly. Our conductor, Mr. Gumbacher, furiously tapped his baton on his music stand until we came to a screeching halt mid-piece. He turned to the audience and to our great embarrassment, shouted, "Folks, that was *lousy*! We'll give it another lick!"

By now demoralized, the Gumbacher symphony Choir this time made the spirited march sound more like a dirge.

Then it was the turn of my chief rival for the audience's approval, Bob Murray. A veteran of three previous concerts, he by that time had completely conquered the intricacies of *Pop Goes the Weasel*. The audience, impressed, shouted "Encore!" But Bob, not ready for any encore just yet, retreated off-stage.

A friend of my parents owned a radio station, Oshkosh's one and only station, devoted to bringing to Oshkosh ears fine classical "electrical transcriptions" eight hours a day on Sundays. My father persuaded him to let me play one selection "live" on his Sunday morning program, "Music to Live by". I had by this time sufficient self-confidence to repeat my first public offering of *Humoresque*, which had earned some applause, but luckily for me, no shouts of "Encore!" at the High School fiasco. My parents, sitting at home to get the full effect of the radio broadcast, were elated when they received a congratulatory call from Miss Rose, my elementary school music teacher. Other than that single call, there were no others, no offers of a Julliard scholarship in the offing. Carnegie Hall seemed more remote than ever, as I entered my second year under Mr. Gumbacher's tutelage. By this time I was working to perfect an abbreviated version of *Liebesleid*. It still lacked the polish and panache of my teacher's favorite rendition, but I was getting close, perhaps for him uncomfortably close. It came dawning on me one fine day that I had reached a plateau, not a very high one, almost to the limited level of my teacher, and that there was no-where to go but straight ahead, pot holes and all, or even downward.

One afternoon my mother on the spur of the moment decided it would be a nice thing for me to play *Liebesleid* for her ladies' bridge group. After much urging and a thinly veiled whispered threat, I gave in, and sulkily began to play my latest special piece. The ladies were talking incessantly, and continuing with their bridge game. Only a few were listening to me play. Fed up with their rudeness, I stopped playing, glared at them, and when they quieted down I resumed playing. But their conversation resumed, even louder than before, as if to try to drown out my efforts. In a moment they have probably always referred to as temporary insanity, I flung my Irish violin with the inlaid shamrocks down onto the floor. The thick oriental rug minimized the damage; only a string or two and the bridge were broken.

A hush came over my audience as I administered a crushing *coup de grace* by stomping its midsection repeatedly into the carpet.

My dashed career as a concert violinist, over the ensuing months, became a daily, unremitting topic of rebuke from my father:

"That's all the thanks we get, all those two-dollar lessons, and that beautiful Irish violin with the shamrocks, all down the drain."

~~~

8.

Hizzoner the Mayor

The Mayor of Oshkosh, George Oaks, was a longtime friend and fellow wine-maker of my father's. He was not a very impressive-looking politician. In this era of television, he wouldn't have been elected assistant dog-catcher. He was short, thin and stooped over, probably from years of kissing babies and patting little kids on the shoulder. His pin-stripe suit was rumpled and worn at the elbows, and his left cheek had a permanent bulge from a plug of chewing tobacco ensconced inside. Nor was he a fervent dévotée of shaving daily.

But Mayor Oaks was a consummate small-town politico. He instinctively knew how to attract and to keep the loyalty of most every segment of our depression-worn town of 39,108 souls. This was a valuable skill in a community where class distinctions ran deep. The north side of the Fox River housed most of the middle and upper middle class, and the south side was mainly blue collar domain, many heavily dependent on relief checks and W.P.A. projects.

Oshkosh's City Hall, where "Hizzoner" the Mayor held sway, reflected his laissez-faire attitude toward appearances. The aged barn-red wooden structure looked as if it dated back to the Civil War era, and could well have had its original coat of paint for the past seventy-five years. I knew its dark, smelly main corridor from frequent Saturday morning visits down that long corridor of power lined with brass spittoons that led to Hizzoner's office at the end of the hall. As a fifteen-year-old political appointee, I had served (without pay, of course) as Oshkosh Bicycle Court Judge in a makeshift Saturday morning courtroom set up in the City Council chambers, alongside the Mayor's office.

The Bicycle Court and its staff of teenaged Bicycle Police was our mayor's favorite project: enforcement of strict bicycle regulations (every bike had to carry a license plate, an operable headlight and tail light, and had to stay off sidewalks, or be summoned to the town's Star Chamber for violators, presided over by myself with the City Attorney advising me and moderating my sentences I meted out, which tended to be draconian).

Every Saturday before court session, I reported to the Mayor's office for a pep talk, and the inevitable pat on my shoulder as I went forth to administer my brand of justice.

"Hizzoner's" office was a study in dust-coated, politically eclectic clutter. Above his high-backed executive chair hung a framed color portrait of President Franklin Delano Roosevelt, and on his desk was an autographed photo of the late President Warren G. Harding. Notable by his absence anywhere in the room was former President Herbert Hoover, who rightly or wrongly bore the blame for the Depression and its awful consequences.

As Bicycle Court presiding Judge, I felt a twinge of hypocrisy and questionable ethics when I used my bicycle to deliver a plain-wrapped box once a week to the Alexian Brothers Hospital. The drugstore, Schroeder's I worked for, on Jackson Drive, marked the wrapper "ice cream", but I was repeatedly warned not to drop the package, which always had a glass bottle inside. Whenever I delivered the "ice cream" to the brown-robed priest at the reception desk, he would manage a jovial wink, as certain as I was of the box's contents. That institution, surrounded by a high wire mesh fence, was dedicated to the treatment of alcoholic priests. Through the fence passersby could watch the then sober robed clerics playing volleyball and croquet.

Having grown up in the era of Prohibition, I had witnessed more than several annual merry processions down into our basement. My father, Mayor Oaks, Police Chief Gabbert, Officer MacDonald, and Officer Copey Hanson, each was carrying large oblong baskets of dark blue grapes and bags of sugar. This annual event was looked forward to by my father and his cronies. The pressing of the grapes, the pouring of the mash into a large oaken barrel, the adding of sugar had almost a ceremonial air about it. They would then leave the cellar, play poker upstairs and let nature do its messy work all winter long. The mash fermented, and the odorous impurities spewed out of the cask until Spring, when, after several months of aging, the young wine was poured into bottles without labels. Future archeologists, finding a deep †-shaped trench etched into our cellar's concrete floor, would probably attribute this phenomenon to some religious rite. I often speculated if that acidy residue could do that to solid concrete, what could it do to one's gullet? At any rate, the gift of these bottles of home-vintnered wine made highly appreciated bridge prizes for my mother's friends, and much-enjoyed refreshment for my father's poker club. One of Oshkosh's most looked forward-to social events, at least among my elementary school teachers, was an annual bridge party my mother gave for all my teachers, past and present, where each received a complimentary bottle of the near-forbidden juice.

My dad always claimed, (which seemed to me even at the time that he was protesting too much) that *technically* no law was broken, since he never sold a single bottle of the Livingstone Cellar's output.

A Call to Arms

My father, after my violent severance of ties with the world of music, deemed that what I needed most was a good dose of military discipline. He invited the commandant of nearby St. John's Military Academy, Colonel Roy C. Farrand, U.S. Army, Ret., to come to our home and interview me as to my suitability, and to discuss the costs of such an education. The old colonel, arriving at the house in a highly polished recent vintage chauffeur-driven Packard, despite his Kentucky-colonel appearance and courtly manners, had wasted his time coming to Oshkosh. My father, even though he longed to own a Cadillac, had the good business sense of not living in an expensive house or not driving a top-of-the-line luxury car. How could a mere director of a small military school afford to be chauffeured around in a Packard? That must come out of the high tuition fees, of that he was certain.

But ever resourceful, my dad had yet another card to play, his friend, Mayor Oaks. In 1940, after the Wisconsin National Guard was federalized and sent to Louisiana, through some adroit political footwork, "Hizzoner" organized a Wisconsin State Guard Infantry Battalion, with its headquarters conveniently located at the local Armory, a former German Athletic Club building named *Turner Verein*. He received a direct commission of Lieutenant Colonel, was made commander of the Battalion, which was modelled after the British Home Guard. The Wisconsin National Guard, in his eyes, left Wisconsin, and Oshkosh in particular defenseless in case of enemy attack, improbable though that might have been at that time or any other time since the Winnebago Indians were pushed into tiny reservations.

"Bending" regulations or municipal ordinances was never an insurmountable obstacle for our mayor. He saw to it that my enlistment papers read "seventeen", the minimum age, even though I wouldn't reach that age until November, six months away.

I was not at all unhappy to exchange violin and bow for rifle and bayonet. I had always had a penchant for things military. In fact, I was keenly disappointed when my father gave thumbs down to my entering St. John's. After all, hadn't I shown considerable military proclivities when the Boy Scouts of America "purged" me for teaching military drill to nine-year-old Cub Scouts?

On my first night at Turner Verein Hall I was issued a World War I Lee Enfield rifle, a bayonet long enough to go through two fat watermelons side by side, a World War I style helmet that resembled a barber's wash basin, an entrenching tool, a rough wool uniform, canvas leggings and all the things that weigh down a soldier's full pack completed my ensemble.

A few weeks after joining the State Guard, an order came down that required us to pack our Lee Enfield rifles in cosmoline and ship them to the United Kingdom which had left on the beach at Dunkirk some 90,000 rifles and five thousand "lorries." To our disgust we were issued instead sporty civilian-looking shotguns. I immediately complained to our battalion commander, the Mayor. For some time he had been observing me on the drill floor, and was impressed, perhaps overly so, with my relatively high standards of "spit and polish" compared to my fellow privates, which wasn't saying all that much.

He listened sympathetically to my complaint about having to carry a shotgun better suited for bird and rabbit hunters.

"Now Jack, as you see, I am required to carry a Colt .45 sidearm. How would you like to carry one also? I'm going to appoint you as my Aide de Camp, and as such, you will no longer have to carry a shotgun, but you'll be issued a .45 pistol, just like mine."

"Aide de Camp!" That elegant-sounding euphemism belied the fact that in actuality I became his orderly, or for want of a more precise term, his "flunky". My new duties consisted of keeping his boots and Sam Brown belt polished, his brass insignia buffed with jeweler's rouge, his service pistol oiled, and his spittoons, strategically placed at intervals along the edge of the drill floor, emptied and burnished.

Being the only enlisted man in the whole battalion allowed to wear a sidearm spawned a torrent of snide remarks from my shotgun-toting fellow soldiers. I ignored the envy and resentment as best I could, having read somewhere that all great military leaders must cope with this problem as they rise to the top.

Colonel Oaks's military appearance on the drill floor improved so dramatically that his officers and men began to emulate his higher standard. His spittoons shone as never before, and the unit even passed a State Inspection, the first time in its history. As a reward our Colonel promised us a "beer bust" on the shores of nearby Lake Butte des Morts (Mound of the dead) at the culmination of weekend-long "war games". Those "war games" were eagerly looked forward to by the rank and file, a once-a-year opportunity to get away from the house, from the wife and kids, from taking out the garbage, and much more comfortable than fishing through the ice during winter.

Our colonel's talent for public relations and logistics was amply demonstrated when at the conclusion of the field exercises, a Chief Oshkosh Brewery truck arrived at just the right time and unloaded barrel after barrel of beer. During our all-night "beer bust", the beer and food never ran out. In a good-natured, alcohol- fueled critique of the "war games", our by now beloved little colonel, standing atop an ammunition box to be seen, declared, in words etched into my memory,

"Gents, we may not have caught any saboteurs at the lake, but we sure sank a lot of schooners!"

I learned much from Colonel Oaks's example in attracting and holding the loyalty of his subordinates, but I never acquired the need for a spittoon.

~~~

9.

The House That Was Never a Home

During the Second World War while stationed in England I had a chance to travel by jeep around the southern counties past some old, imposing estates. The vast houses, often situated far off the road yet clearly in view, symbolized for me the aloofness, privilege of the landed gentry. As is the case with many an old, elegant lady, the wear and tear of the passage of years are all the more evident the closer you look.

There was one particular Tudor mansion in Wiltshire I once passed by that sparked a strong feeling of *déjà vue.* That cream-colored great front window with its many panes and the tall, proud elms in front, could I have once seen it in a film, or in a dream? No. A sudden synopsis clicked in and told me that it was no more than a look-alike of the Paine mansion back in Oshkosh, with its great front window looking out on Algoma Boulevard. During the middle 'thirties I had often ridden past the place on my bike. I had seen it rise from the ground in fits and starts over several years, and once it was finished, there were delivery trucks unloading big wooden crates which were carried inside the house and stored in the great hall, gathering cobwebs through the years.

The estate, with its lavish display of rose gardens, when finally completed, housed shipments from all over Europe of furnishings and objets d'art personally selected by Nathan Paine and his wife Jessie Kimberly Paine. But the mansion's owners never lived in it, and for good reason. Local folklore insists, and with ample supporting evidence, that the Paine Lumber Company, which sprawled along the Fox River just a few hundred yards from the mansion, after the Crash of 1929 faltered, then closed, throwing more than 1600 employees out of work. The workers, many immigrant laborers from Germany and Poland, lived and worked under hazardous working conditions with extremely low pay. The Paine Lumber Company even employed young children who should have been in school. Many were obliged to live in a dingy row of company-owned tenements down along the river, practically within sight of the Paines' new mansion. They were inveigled to deposit their savings in the Paine Thrift Bank, and when it closed, not only their meager savings were wiped out, but they discovered they were held financially responsible for the bank's deficits. Those depression years brought back to the workers' minds memories of their ill-fated attempt to strike against the company back in 1894, when the Paine Company called in the State Militia to break up the strike. The Paines' temerity and bad judgement to pore into their future "home" more than $800,000 (in real depression dollars) within a few hundred yards of their company-owned tenements created much resentment.

It was common knowledge that once the house was completed, the workers sent the Paines a note threatening to blow up the house if they ever moved into it.

All during the depression years you could see through the corner gate into the great window a mountain of wooden crates filled with the Paines' costly acquisitions. My father was indignant. "What a waste! They were galavanting around Europe on a shopping spree after their bank failed.

44

How the Paines ever thought they could come back to Oshkosh is beyond me!"

The Paine Lumber company left a legacy of resentment spawned by generations of ten-hour, six-day work weeks under appalling working conditions. Needless to say, after her husband's death in Florida in 1947, Mrs. Paine chose to move as far away from Oshkosh as she could, settling in La Jolla, California.

In fairness to the Paines, after their deaths it came to light that they had been frequent and generous contributors to local charities and churches. Perhaps it was out of guilt feelings that they were trying to make amends for their selfish, paternalistic treatment of their workers. Mrs. Paine, in her will, left the estate to the City of Oshkosh. In 1948 the house and grounds, converted into the Paine Art Center and Arboretum opened its doors to the public with a close Paine relative, George Paine Nevitt in charge.

For the past fifty years it's been "payback time" for the late Mr. and Mrs. Paine. The house, never their home, has fulfilled a better, fuller purpose.

~~~

10.

Lewis Hine, A Photographer for the Twentieth Century

Although Oshkosh's now famous photographer, Lewis Hine died in poverty and obscurity in 1940, his poignant, darkly brooding photographs of child laborers during the early 1900's have recently been commemorated by the U.S. Postal Service, issuing a stamp featuring a photo he made in 1907 of a child laborer. That photo was one of hundreds he made during his travels throughout the country under the auspices of the National Child Labor Committee early in the century.

While Hine was living in Oshkosh, he must have been painfully aware of the many unschooled, malnourished children who toiled for pennies an hour in the huge Paine Lumber Company that sprawled along the log-choked Fox river.

A public previously unaware or uncaring about the exploitation of children in the nation's factories, mills and mines finally goaded the Congress of the United States to enact meaningful, merciful Child Labor laws.

Hine's work on occasion has inspired me to use my camera as an instrument of social protest, to pique the viewer's interest and concern for some of our society's most blatant faults, needful of attention and correction. Through the past thirty years I have built up a collection photos of signs which reflect many of our foibles and shortcomings. The collection is called "Signs of the Times".

Hine's pictures of a lamentable bygone era of child breadwinners cannot be diluted by the passage of the years, once you have seen them. Even today they convey the same poignant emotional impact that they had when they were first published. They remind me of how Dickens' *Oliver Twist* and Steinbeck's *Of Mice and Men* affected me when I read them as an adolescent.

Appreciation and recognition of Hine as a photographer came, as is so often the case, posthumously, but he left a great body of work for other photographers to emulate, even in these more enlightened times. After all, there never has been a society so perfect as not to need improvement and reform.

~~~

11.
A Long-time Local Hero

During my high school years I used to cycle to the Oshkosh Public Library to do my homework assignments. On the way I liked to stop for a Coke at the Schroeder Drugstore downtown. It was a popular gathering place of the town's leading businessmen and professionals for coffee and conversation. I often saw a tall, thin lantern-jawed man with thick spectacles, always accompanied by admiring friends. Sylvester Wittman, or Steve, as he preferred to be called, by the late nineteen thirties was already nationally known as an "old-timer" in aviation. He was a quiet, outgoing, affable man who wore his mantle of a national champion air racer, aircraft designer and builder of experimental racing planes with self-effacing humility.

On Sundays I used to pester my parents to take me out to the local airport where I could usually find Steve tinkering with his latest home-designed and built stubby-winged little racer, either "Bonzo" or "Chief Oshkosh". His little flying contraptions and his iron-nerved piloting established speed records at many of the nation's leading air races, the Cleveland and the Thompson among them.

During the Second World War, Steve, under contract with the Army Air Corps, trained hundreds of Army Air Cadet corps pilots. His trainees logged over seventy thousand flying hours, equivalent to a million four hundred thousand miles without a single serious accident or injury.

A Long-time Local Hero

Still flying his own plane in 1995 at the age of ninety-one, and having had several brushes with death in near-accidents while racing, it seemed that the old pilot would never stop flying. But in late April, 1995 Steve and his wife Paula, flying in his own Wittman-designed aircraft, were on their way back to Oshkosh from their winter home in Ocala, Florida, when their plane disintegrated in mid-air over rugged hilly terrain in northeastern Alabama. Their bodies were recovered on April 30th.

Oshkosh had a true pioneer in aviation, who began as a barnstormer in an old World War I Army trainer in the nineteen twenties. One of his racing planes, "Buster" is displayed alongside Lindbergh's "Spirit of St. Louis" at the National Aeronautics and Space Museum in the Smithsonian Institution in Washington, D.C.. The old airport has been named after him. Wittman Field hosts hundreds of thousands of American Experimental Aircraft Association attendees there during their big meets every August. Steve put Oshkosh on the map as a town with something unique and special to offer.

~~~

12.

Where's Pearl Harbor?

It was a cold, but sunny weekend in December, 1941. My dad had warmed up the car, scraped a layer of ice off the windows, tossed a couple of blankets into our 1940 Chrysler and announced, "We're going to watch the ice boat races."

Menomonee Park sprawled along the west shore of our thirty-mile by eight-mile inland freshwater sea, Lake Winnebago. Out on the ice of our big, frozen lake were up to a hundred out-house-looking portable wooden shacks that sheltered shivering ice fishermen as they sat for hours on end looking at holes in the ice, hoping to spear or snag a northern pike or a white bass, swilling down thermoses of hot coffee laced with "schnaps". Several hundred yards farther out on the lake a fleet of sleek, swift iceboats flitted silently by at speeds approaching ninety miles an hour. Several years before, according to a National Geographic article, the world's speed record for iceboats was set on our lake, a bewildering 135 miles per hour.

My parents, classical music buffs, were listening to a string quartet concert coming out of Chicago, on the car radio. The ensemble, broadcasting from the Empire Room of the Palmer House, was playing an appropriate selection that morning: *Hymn to the Sun.*

Their performance was interrupted by a long pause, then a terse announcement: " We interrupt this broadcast to bring you a special news bulletin. Pearl Harbor is under attack by Japanese planes! We will keep you informed as we receive more information. Now, back to the Palmer House. Stay tuned to WGN."

Dad and mother looked at each other quizzically, then at me. My dad, having left after one year of high school to help support his widowed mother, never had been introduced to much in the way of geography or history. Mother, on the other hand, who had the benefit of a Texas small town high school graduation diploma, gave a shrug, not attempting to guess.

"Don't look at me," I demurred, "I've never heard of the place before."

As the music resumed, my dad, impatient, shouted, "Where in hell is Pearl Harbor?"

A few minutes later the announcer broke in and with strident tones, sounding more like a sportscaster at a major league game, proclaimed, "At this very moment in a sneak attack without a declaration of war, Japanese planes are continuing to drop bombs on our fleet anchored at Pearl Harbor."

"Turn to another station, dear," my mother said, maybe there's someone who knows where Pearl Harbor is."

It then struck me that if our ships were being attacked, we were going to fight back, and declared war or not, our country was now at war. My future in the military was assured!

The announcer broke in again. "The President will address a joint session of Congress tomorrow, to declare that a state of war exists between the United States and the Japanese Empire," a somber Kaltenborn announced.

Meanwhile, the ice fishermen sat in their shacks, and the ice boats flitted by as if there were no such place as Pearl Harbor.

Jake's Departure

As I walked to school the following day, eager as I was to get to school and share in the excitement about Pearl Harbor, I noticed three big men leave a car parked in front of Jake the Barber's little shop on Main Street. As they entered the shop, Jake was finishing brushing the floor as they read to him from a paper. Then Jake put on his coat and hat, walked up to his old wind-up cash register in the window, took out all the cash, and pressed the "No Sale" key. Accompanied by the men, he locked his front door, and rode away with them.

That was the last time Jake the Barber, a native of Dusseldorf, one of the town's noisiest Nazi sympathizers, was ever seen again, at least in Oshkosh. Five years later, home from the war, I drove by his shop. The "No Sale" sign still graced the cash register in the window.

~~~

13.

Perchance to Dream

It lasted only a few seconds. I've never regarded it as "just a bad dream." It was much more than that. It was so full of details, so real! I still recall it as if it happened last night, that terror I felt one night back in 1943. During all the years that have followed, that dream's message has continued to haunt me.

I was seventeen at the time, and had just enlisted in the Army Reserve. Eager to escape my hometown and to see the world, I was impatiently waiting for my call-up to begin basic training, to be delivered from my depressing, boring hometown.

An old guidebook described Oshkosh as "The Fair White City by the Winnebago Sea." The city was *white* alright, ninety-nine and forty-four one-hundredths percent white, Anglo-Saxon, Teutonic, Slavic white. Our town boasted a tiny sliver of racial diversity: one "colored" family, the Shads, whose daughter, Gertrude, was our family maid when I was in kindergarten. I loved to show her off to my envious school mates as she walked me to school. There was one Chinese family, the Lems, who provided Oshkosh palates with the best and only Chinese cuisine in town. And then there was "Mexican Bill," a wiry little old codger with bowed legs who always wore a weather-beaten straw cowboy hat. He exercised and groomed about a dozen horses at the town's stable at the north end of town. The horses were the same proud animals that supported the considerable bulk of Oshkosh's Finest, Police Chief Gabbert and his cohorts at every fourth of July parade. They also served the Carver Dairy Company, providing the locomotion for their fleet of milk wagons.

Oshkosh offered little in the way of adventure or excitement to a seventeen-year-old brought up on a steady diet of radio land's *Jack Armstrong, All-American Boy, Terry and the Pirates, the Lone Ranger* and *Gangbusters*.

The Air Corps came to town in 1943 and set up barracks for a couple of hundred air cadets in my old Rose C. Swart Grammar School classrooms. The town began to shake off its depression-induced torpor when orders came flowing in for tank axles, signal corps reels, uniforms and G.I. (3.2%) beer. For the first time the strange accents of New Yorkers, Alabamans and Texans were heard on the streets of Oshkosh, and in its neighborhood taverns. I was to discover, to my amazement, that a New Yorker wasn't necessarily a racketeer or a gangster, as *Gang Busters* of radio fame had led me to believe. Likewise, a Texan drawl didn't automatically make its owner a rustler or a gun-fighter.

A bit of excitement shook the town in June, 1943. It happened on the eve of my graduation from high school. As a result of a too-loosely chaperoned cottage party on the shore of Lake Butte des Morts, one or two of the less fortunate attendees got pregnant. Their teacher chaperone resigned from the faculty and joined the WAC's, and the girls' alleged impregnators were banished from any further affiliation with the Order of DeMolay.

But for sheer excitement, nothing could compare with my dream. A few months before being called to active duty, in 1943, I awoke, shaken as never before or since, by a dream: I was marched up to a post, tied to it, and faced a firing squad made up of dirty, unshaven soldiers, led by an officer wearing a starched light blue cotton uniform. The pock-marked wall behind me was of adobe, topped by shards of broken bottle glass. The officer pinned a piece of paper on the center of my shirt, and ordered the squad to aim and to fire. As the bullets tore through my body and into the wall behind me, I awoke, shaking uncontrollably, and drenched in sweat.

Not wanting to alarm my parents, who already were worrying about their son, the soldier, I decided to keep any mention of the dream to myself, except for Mrs. LeDoyt.

Mrs. LeDoyt, who had a reputation as a clairvoyant, a "seer," lived down the street from my home. Her talent, her "gift," as she called it, was well-known, even as far away as Chicago. It wasn't unusual to see chauffeured limousines bearing Illinois license plates parked in front of her shabby, unpainted house on Lincoln Avenue. I felt she, if anyone, could tell me the meaning of that terrible dream that had left me so terrified. I had absolute faith in her powers. She once solved the disappearance of a family heirloom, a gold brooch. She came to our house one day, and over tea and sandwiches told my mother, "There's no loss! Somebody, not family, hid it in a can, a can full of little holes. It's nearby, somewheres in this house! Whoever took it got scared, and is waitin' for the right time, when you've stopped frettin' 'bout it, to get it out of the house."

I was standing in the doorway, fascinated. Mrs. LeDoyt peered at me through her thick spectacles that made her eyes look twice as big and said, "Jack, 'member the day you fell off of your bike in front of my house and came to my door covered with fresh tar? 'Member what I told you? You've got a Third Eye, and that's for sure!"

My mother was intrigued. "What's this about a Third Eye?" She asked.

Mrs. LeDoyt smiled. "It's nuthin' to fret about, that's for sure. It's a gift, a gift from the Good Lord. Not many people have it, but your son's got it, and that's for sure. It'll protect him through thick and thin, no matter what comes his way."

A few weeks after Mrs. LeDoyt's visit, my mother was cleaning out an old cedar chest in the attic. She came upon a perforated can filled with mothballs, opened it, and found the missing brooch. Our maid was sent packing home to Rhinelander.

I just *knew* that if anyone could tell me what that dream meant, it was Mrs. LeDoyt. I went to her house early one morning before any limousines would arrive. She opened her door, put down her carpet sweeper and said, "I been expectin' you. Come on in and tell me 'bout it."

"Please promise me you won't tell my folks about it, about this dream I had. They musn't worry about me any more than they do already, what with me going into the army soon and all."

She gave an affirmative nod, and to reinforce it, she touched her lips and gave them a little twist, signifying that her lips were sealed. Then, looking at me through those thick glasses, she said, "Now you jest tell me ever'thing you 'member, dear."

I recalled for her all I could, and as I ended my account, I was shaking and gasping for breath. Mrs. LeDoyt's eyes were closed. Then with a jerky movement, as if aroused out of a sound sleep, she said with great deliberateness, "Pay no 'tention to that dream! It's somethin' well, somethin' that happened to you a long time ago, in another body. Now don't try to make me 'splain all this, it's too complicated. Just 'member, Jack, that it don't mean it has to happen again. All the same, it's a kinda warnin' if you make the same mistake again."

"What kind of mistake? I don't understand!" I interjected. Mrs. LeDoyt, now calm and smiling, squeezed my hand to reassure me. "Jest trust in the Good Lord, but don't you go 'round stickin' your neck out. Don't be a coward, but don't try to be no hero, neither. Just be a good soldier, don't take any fool chances, and you'll come out just fine. Now you mind what I just told you, y'hear?"

She stood up, and I understood this to mean the session was over. Relieved, yet still perplexed, I thanked her and asked, awkwardly, how much I owed her. She grabbed her sweeper and started to push it toward me as if to chase me out the door.

"Oh, shaw, your folks were so good to Henry before he died, all that carpenter work around your house, you don't owe me a penny. Now, git!"

~~~

14.

Why Not The Navy?

Why had I enlisted in the Army Enlisted Reserve Corps at the age of seventeen? This didn't happen without a lot of "selling" to my parents by the recruiting sergeant, for their written consent was required. My mother, tears brimming in her eyes, finally signed the document, mumbling to herself, "I didn't raise my boy to be a soldier." The recruiter accomplished this minor miracle by telling them, "Look at it this way, folks. Your son will be drafted anyway after his eighteenth birthday, and now that they're drafting kids into the Navy, he wants to avoid that if at all possible. Besides, he has the whole summer to get a college semester under his belt. That will look good for him on his service record, and will probably get him into some training program designed for bright young guys like Jack."

Why my horror of being drafted into the Navy? After all, even then I was willing to concede that the Navy offered a few advantages over the Army: a girl in every port, the thrill of sinking enemy submarines, and coffee at all hours of the day and night. But my misadventures in the Sea Scouts of America did nothing to endear me to anything remotely resembling a life at sea, or for boats, for that matter. Above all else, I had never been able to learn to swim, or even to float. There must have been too much lead in my bones, I figured. I was therefore eminently unsuited to serve aboard an oil-reeking boat surrounded by water, with sharks all around and underneath.

Not the least of my objections was the ridiculous "sailor suits" the Navy made the enlisted men wear.

Why, then had I joined the Sea Scouts in the first place? I have to regress for a moment to the age of fifteen, when I was forced to resign from the Boy Scouts of America for being too "militaristic," after having been caught teaching my "den" of nine-year-old Cub Scouts military drill. A family friend, Art Kannenberg, curator of our local museum, had lent me a half-dozen rusty old carbines captured from the Spaniards in Cuba during the Spanish-American War. They were just the right size for my "cubs." I had gotten hold of an old War Department manual on military drill, and studied it until I knew I could teach my kids military drill. The cubs had mastered the intricacies of "Present Arms," "Order Arms," and "Right Shoulder, Arms."

Word of my accomplishment reached the desk of the local Boy Scouts of America executive, Harry Hertz. He paid a surprise visit to our drill session, and I was caught in the act. Instead of a pat on the back, or even a medal, what I got was Mr. Hertz's admonition, "Jack, you can't go on teaching military drill in the BSA. We're not a military organization."

My protests and offer to show Mr. Hertz how proud my cubs were of their achievement made no impression whatsoever. I was warned, "You have to stop the military drill or you'll have to resign from the BSA. It's all up to you."

I chose what I considered then as now, the only honorable way out. I resigned my position as Den Chief, and left the BSA. Word that I got kicked out of the BSA, "purged," was bound to get around Oshkosh, so in order to head off those ugly rumors, I immediately joined the Sea

Scouts, not that I was all that fond of water. In the Sea Scouts I soon learned to hate boats.

I had a presentment that someday a biographer, digging into my past history would find the seeds of an illustrious military career having been planted by my old friend, Art Kannenberg, only to be uprooted, only temporarily, by Harry Hertz.

Since I was labelled "unteachable" as far as swimming was concerned, the "Skipper" of our Sea Scout "ship" (the "ship" being a leaky old hand-me-down sloop that could still float with ten boys aboard) - decreed that I could only board the boat if I were incased in a bulky "Mae West" life jacket. My "shipmates" taunted and teased me so much on my first (and very last) "cruise" on Lake Winnebago, that I kept to myself, sitting astride the boat's centerboard box. The first hard lesson I learned was that when the Skipper shouted "coming about!" It meant for me to duck low to avoid being clouted on the side of my head by a swinging mainsail boom. Being an uninitiated landlubber, I didn't heed the Skipper's order, much to my regret. Another even more painful lesson occurred later that day as we headed back to the harbor. In shallow water the hinged sheet-metal centerboard struck a submerged rock, which pushed up the centerboard through the centerboard box with such force that looking back on it now, it's a miracle that I ever became a father to six daughters.

So my aversion to things nautical has strong underpinnings, so to speak.

Having succeeded in getting my parents' permission to join the Army's Enlisted Reserve Corps (ERC), I thought a celebration was in order. I asked Dad to drive us out to the A&W Root Beer stand, and with my own allowance, treated them to a giant five-cent frosted mug of root beer and a ten-cent hamburger each. "After all," I explained to them, "I'll soon be making twenty-one dollars a month, which will be coming in like clockwork."

That night I thanked God profusely for having saved me from the Navy. Then I asked Him, "Dear Lord, could I please be sent to Europe instead of to the Pacific?" (Wisconsin's old National Guard 32nd Division was contributing heavily to the casualty lists coming out of the Pacific Theater.) Besides, who'd want to see New Guinea? Anyway, Europe held a special attraction for me, ever since the eighth grade. Our teacher, Miss Scott had hung over her blackboard a framed five-foot sepia-toned panoramic photograph of the famous Druid stone monuments at Stonehenge, in England. I always hoped that someday I would walk among those mysterious stones.

There was an even more powerful lure: France. My near-obsession to see and savor France owes its beginning to Commencement Day, back in 1938, when as valedictorian of my graduating ninth grade class I had just completed an impassioned, nervously delivered oration. As I stepped down from the stage, a beautiful, olive-complexioned lady, the mother of my fellow student, Jacqueline Waite, rushed up to congratulate me, giving me a warm hug and a kiss on both cheeks. Her delightful French accent and the light fragrance of her perfume fulled me with admiration for all things French. I had always had an aversion to perfume ever since my encounter with Madame Schuman-Heink at the train station back in 1928 (which I have related in an earlier chapter). But Mrs. Waite's *Canal Number Five* or whatever it was bewitched me. My parents, who witnessed her Gallic congratulatory gesture, told me that Mrs. Waite was a World War One war bride brought to Oshkosh by Mr. Waite, a veteran of the war.

"How could they keep her down in Paree, once she had seen Oshkosh?" My father quipped.

Ever since that delightfully tactile and olfactory experience with Mrs. Waite, not only did I nourish a determination to stay out of the swamps of New Guinea, but an equally obsessive desire to see Paris. Certainly, an omniscient God saw through my thinly-veiled ulterior motive for having asked for Europe, but knowing how boys will be boys, I was sure He would understand.

~~~

15.

A Day in The Life of A Buck Private

In April, 1944 Tom Gabriel, from Appleton, Wisconsin and my second cousin Morton Lee Gazerwitz from Oshkosh and I were in the home stretch of hellish basic training at a sweltering army post near the Mexican border, Fort Bliss, Texas. Fort Bliss: an oxymoron if ever there was one.

After "falling in" for 6:00 a.m. reveille and "falling out" for a breakfast of powdered eggs, paraffin-like tropical butter, powdered milk, laced, we were told, with salpeter to mass-moderate our libidos, and "s--t on a shingle," otherwise known as creamed beef on toast, we were "double-timed" back to our barracks and ordered to "fall in" in ten minutes in full field pack, steel helmet, half a pup tent wrapped around a blanket, cartridge belt, first aid packet, gas mask, a filled canteen, bayonet and scabbard, entrenching tool, mess kit and M-I rifle.

A shrill whistle summoned us to "fall in" to face yet another day of desert training, for the last of our scheduled fourteen-mile hikes into the snake and scorpion-infested "boonies." Even as early as April, the weather had been getting noticeably warmer. An ominous sign for us that day: a long line of ambulances that formed at the end of our column of some eight hundred young men, or for want of a better word, "trainees."

By noon we had reached the half-way point and were met by field kitchens which had been set up in advance of our arrival. On a day already pushing up into the 'eighties, the sight of hot, greasy pork chops swimming in gravy and mashed potatoes in our steel mess kits didn't seem particularly enticing, especially when the gleam of the grease was dulled by wind-borne dust. It was on days such as this that Tom and Morton Lee would give me side-long glances as if to say, "See what you've gotten me into!" I had talked them into enlisting in the ERC a year before.

By mid-day the water in our canteens was more like tepid bath water. After a dessert of warm tapioca the medics came around and distributed salt pills, promising us they would prevent heat stroke.

My teeth still had a gritty residue of the sand-blown gravy and tapioca. The time to let off steam about the "chow," I thought, was long past due. I complained to anyone who would listen, "This sludge they call 'chow' isn't fit for human consumption. Army cooks must get special training to make food taste this bad."

My fellow trainees, in an effort to shut me up, pretended to shoo pesky flies away from their mouths. It didn't dawn on me that my tirade was being overheard by the "old man," our battalion commander, who was standing just behind me. I felt a sharp tap of a stick on my shoulder. It was our colonel's riding crop, a vestige of his years in the old horse cavalry.

"What th' hell's the mattah with this chow? Lemme taste it! It's the same chow I et, an' if it's good 'nough fo' me, it's good 'nough fo' mah men!" He grabbed my mess kit and spoon and sampled my "chow."

A Day in The Life of A Buck Private

The rules of military courtesy furthest from my mind, I stayed squatting in the sand and didn't look up at him as I shouted back, "Well, sir, that all depends on what you're used to at home."

Everyone around me cringed as the colonel walked up to the First Sergeant and whispered something in his ear. Snake patrol or latrine duty was in my immediate future. Then the "old man" turned on his heel and climbed back into his jeep.

As we resumed our hike, our steel helmets were getting too hot to touch. It was like sticking our heads into a cauldron.

My quart-sized canteen was emptied as I savored the last few drops of hot water. Each step ahead became more exhausting than the one before. As the temperature climbed into the 'nineties, some of the older men started to drop along the roadside, to be collected by the medics and loaded into ambulances for a trip back to the post hospital.

Feeling dizzy and faint, I was barely aware of my staggering away from the column, into the desert. I was trying to reach a tall glass of cold beer, just beyond my grasp. Our platoon leader, a brand-new little "second looie" with a Napoleonic complex, ran up to me and tried to pull me back into the column. That's all I remember until I woke up in the Post Hospital. They treated me for heat exhaustion and dehydration, kept me overnight, and discharged me the next morning, just in time for our Saturday morning inspection. The First Sergeant, shocked at how I looked, didn't have the heart to make me stand at attention alongside my cot for the inspection. Instead, he had me laid out on my cot like a corpse, ordering me to "lay at attention, and don't move a muscle."

After the inspection I was treated like a hero. My fellow privates, as it turned out, had witnessed a crime I had committed in my delirium: I had landed a solid haymaker on our "ninety-day wonder's" jaw when he tried to pull me back into the column. I had visions of facing a court martial, my army career up for grabs, pleading not guilty by reason of temporary insanity. But nothing came of my violation of the Articles of War except to receive an invitation, good-natured, to "put on the gloves" behind the barracks with my platoon leader, an invitation which I didn't take seriously.

~~~

16.

A Year of Awe and Excitement

Any knowledge I have of Russian history may be attributed to a chance meeting with two people: Sir Bernard Pares, Professor Emeritus of Russian History, London University, and New York Socialite Gloria Vanderbilt. Thanks to these two special people, though more than fifty years have intervened, I've remained fascinated, to the point of obsessed with history's greatest woman, Catherine the Great.

History's greatest woman? You may well ask. What about Cleopatra, Helen of Troy, Marilyn Monroe or Hillary Clinton? As my old friend Sir Bernard Pares would have put it, "Any comparison of Catherine the Great with any other woman in history would be pure piffle, poppycock and balderdash."

My first chance meeting took place during the 1943 Summer session at the University of Wisconsin. As I was approaching the university's impressive Memorial Union building I noticed a bent-over, slight, late seventyish man wearing a rumpled black pinstripe suit and a sweat-stained grey fedora busily lancing bits of candy wrappers and cigarette butts on the lawn in front of the building. He wielded a stick with a pin in its end with great precision, making every thrust count, and he deposited the debris into a brown paper sack.

"What a sad way to make a living," I said to myself, as I entered the ground-floor Ratskeller.

Moments later, as I was carrying my mug of beer and hamburger to a table, I noticed that the old gentleman had sat down across the aisle from me. He looked lonely.

"Mind if I join you?" I asked.

"Not at all, young man. And who might you be?"

"I'm John Livingstone, from Oshkosh, just here for the summer semester before I go into the army."

"Pares, Bernard. My card, young man."

The card proclaimed that he was Professor Emeritus, former head of the Department of Slavonic Studies at London University, and after his name, the initials K.B.E. A knight of the British Empire! This being the first knight I ever had and probably never would again have a mug of beer and a hamburger with, I was overcome with awe and excitement.

My curiosity, not to be denied, prodded me into gingerly broaching the subject of his present occupation. " I couldn't help noticing how expertly you were wielding your lance out in front on the lawn, Sir Bernard."

"Oh, that! I have a penchant for tidiness. Your university has such lovely grounds, don't you know? I was just doing my bit to keep it so."

Sir Bernard's crisp consonants and broad vowels assured me that he was an Englishman of posh background and education, recent evidence to the contrary notwithstanding.

"Tell me, Professor, are you doing research here?"

"Oh, no, just a series of consultations with several universities on establishing departments of Russian studies. I've been sent here by my government. See here, young man. I've been asked to give a lecture on Catherine the Great next week. If you're interested, you're welcome to attend."

Having been invited to attend a lecture by a Knight of the Realm, I was again filled with awe and excitement.

"Having had only a tiny touch of information about Catherine the Great during my high school years, all I remember was that she ruled for a long time, and that they called her The Seraminus of the North."

Sir Bernard smiled, and said, "And you shall learn a lot more about history's greatest woman if you attend the lecture."

I thanked him profusely and promised to attend the lecture.

"Something has bewildered me ever since it happened," I said, "The alliance between Hitler and Stalin. How could two such men, who must have hated one another, become allies?"

Sir Bernard took a took a sip of his beer, shook his head slowly as if to let me know what he was thinking, "*What dolts come across my path.*"

"I shall answer that by posing a simple question: If you know your neighbor is preparing to attack you, and at the time your own defenses are not ready, what would you do?"

I thought long and hard, and came up with, "I'd stall as long as possible to build up my defenses."

"There, you see? You have answered your own question." Sir Bernard's Socratic method summed up in a few words what an hour-long lecture would have accomplished.

"Is it true that Stalin, like all his predecessors, keeps control through terror?"

"Not all his predecessors can be said to have been as cruel and despotic as he is. There are a few notable exceptions, the most notable of all being Catherine the Great, as you shall learn from my lecture."

The lecture hall was filled to capacity, with standing room only. Sir Bernard's quiet, authoritative voice intoned, ". . . born Sophia-Augusta Frederika, Princess of Anhalt-Zerbst, a petty little Prussian principality, she was recruited at the age of fifteen to go to Russia to become betrothed to Grand Duke Peter, nephew of Empress Elizabeth of Russia. Peter, sixteen-year old heir to the throne, was a sadistic, degenerate, stupid, alcoholic nincompoop eminently unsuited for his future role as Tsar, which Catherine was quick to apprehend. His incessant violin playing, drunken bouts with his Guards officers, and the barking and stench of a pack of hounds he kept in an adjoining room did little to endear him to his bride. Catherine early in her marriage came to the conclusion, shared by most of her courtiers, that for the good of Russia, Peter's reign should be mercifully short.

She had endeared herself to the Russian people by abandoning her Lutheran faith for the Russian Orthodox faith, and at the time of the death of Empress Elizabeth, by prolonged and apparently sincere displays of grief at the funeral in December, 1761. While the obsequies were going on, Peter cavorted openly with his coarse, ugly mistress and his fellow drunks, while plotting to banish Catherine to a convent and install in her place his ignorant, uncouth mistress. Catherine, having been apprised of this, decided the time was propitious to depose her husband, the new Tsar Peter III. Nor did she find enthusiastic support wanting among his own Guards regiments, and her lover, Guards Captain Gregory Orlov. . . .Catherine, not a knowing participant in Peter's abdication by strangulation, felt free to ascend the throne, bypassing her young son, Paul, whom she considered to share his father's dubious attributes to rule."

"In a festive, carnival atmosphere immediately after the announcement of Peter's demise 'by a severe attack of hemorrhoids,' the people of Russia expressed their joy in weeks-long drinking bouts which culminated in breaking into liquor stores and warehouses and the looting of all the remaining vodka. The new Tsaritza prudently reimbursed the shopkeepers for their losses, and rewarded handsomely the Guards officers, who, along with her lover, Gregory Orlov, had carried out the coup.

Her co-conspirators' loyalty was assured by Catherine's generous favors and monetary awards, all to the benefit of the landed gentry, at the expense of the already overburdened peasants and serfs. A widespread rebellion against her was ultimately quelled, and its architect, a Cossack brigand named Pugachev, through Catherine's intercession, was beheaded *first*, *then* quartered, Catherine having mercifully reversed the order of the original sentence."

"Catherine had numerous lovers, some twenty officially recognized. Each one, they were to discover, was always completely subservient to her whims and wishes, except for her secret, morganatic husband, Gregory Potemkim."

I thought to myself, (What a fantastic woman! If only we had a president like that!). Of course, I was a callow youth of seventeen when that thought had occurred to me.

A year later I was in the army, stationed at an anti-aircraft artillery position out on Long Island Sound, at Westhampton beach, doing my little bit to defend the greater New York area from German bombers. One warm August evening, there being no imminent threat of an air attack, my army buddy, Tom Gabriel and I were walking toward an old Victorian house the grateful inhabitants of West Hampton Beach had turned into a USO Club. A sedan passed us and came to a stop a few yards ahead. The driver called to us: "Would you like a ride into New York?" Those were the days when accepting a ride from strangers was not particularly fraught with danger, either in New York or Oshkosh.

"Sure, thanks!" I said, and as we got into the car, the driver introduced his wife, a beautiful young brunette about our age: "This is my wife, Gloria Vanderbilt DiCicco, and I'm Pat."

She turned to us and said, "We're staying out on Long Island at a beach house for a few more weeks, and we hope to have your unit come for a beach party soon."

Having never before been invited to a beach party by one of the nation's leading socialites, Tom and I were filled with awe and excitement.

"That's certainly nice of you. We'll all be looking forward to it," Tom answered. (It was just their way of showing how much they appreciated our being there to knock down any German bombers that dared to attack greater New York.)

Mrs. Vanderbilt DiCicco had a couple of theatre tickets in her hand. "Would you boys like to see a Broadway show? It's at the Shubert Theatre. We can let you out in front."

Having never before been given free tickets to a Broadway Show, we were again filled with awe and excitement.

The play turned out to be a spoof on Catherine the Great, written by and starring the not so great Mae West. The tiny actress, clumping about the stage in heavy trailing robes and high platform shoes, never seemed to miss a particular floorboard on the stage, which groaned and creaked as she trod upon it. Miss West's appalling lack of scholarship escaped Tom completely, but not me, and I'm sure Sir Bernard would have been horrified had he been there. When Mae West launched into a long monologue about how she was going to free the serfs and distribute the land to them, I had enough, and said to Tom, "This is pure piffle, poppycock and balderdash. Come on, let's leave during the intermission."

My buddy, not having benefited from the thorough grounding in that phase of Russian history as I had derived from Sir Bernard's lecture, was determined to see it through to the end. It turned out that we were rewarded for staying, when, after the final curtain, Catherine the Great, noticing the great number of servicemen in the audience, graciously invited us all to "Come up and see me on stage," where she gave some of us (me included) a warm hug and grandly presented us with a small autographed photo of herself in one of her most flamboyant costumes. Having never before been hugged by America's foremost practitioner of salacious humor, I was filled with awe and excitement once again.

Before we could be convulsed with awe and excitement by the promised beach party, Uncle Sam shipped us off to the United Kingdom.

~~~

17.
A Cruise to Remember

Having chosen the Army, I had reassured myself that my feet would always feel terra firma beneath them. But one cold night in November, 1944, more than a thousand of us found ourselves packed into the holds of a round-bottomed Caribbean cruise ship, the Grace Line's Santa Paula, designed to carry some three hundred passengers. That first hour on board, the ship hadn't even left the dock at South Boston Harbor when I felt the pangs of nausea creeping up on me.

That same night our battalion chaplain came down below decks to distribute Last Wills and Testaments to each of us for our signatures.

"Where are we headed?" I asked.

Our chaplain smiled and intoned, "Only God knows."

Once out to sea, the merciless Atlantic tossed the Santa Paula around like a cork. We were told that since there were German submarine "wolf packs" looking for our convoy, there was to be no dumping of tell-tale garbage overboard, so that we had better get used to the aroma of orange and banana peels, cigarette butts, all of which combined with the odor of more than a thousand seldom-washed bodies (there being no salt-water soap available for us "steerage" passengers) subsisting in close sardine-like proximity, and the ever-present stench of *mal de mer* vomit all contributed to making that a highly olfactory voyage.

For the first ten days, all we could guess as to our possible destination was that we were travelling in a south-easterly direction, which must surely mean that we would land somewhere in North Africa.

My bunk was the top one, four bunks up from the floor, with about ten inches from the tip of my nose to the steel bulkhead above me. Some unfeeling fellow G.I. had hung from the bulkhead over my bunk by a string a mess kit spoon. Its gyrations and swaying was a constant reminder of the ship's pitching and rolling in the heavy mid-winter seas.

Sergeant Vincent DeCiucis, "V.D." for short, a man with more compassion than all my "buddies" put together, took it upon himself to half-carry me up the ladders to the open deck, so that I could get some fresh air, and so that I was able to stand in line for some thirty minutes to be "fed" a hot dog, an orange and crackers.

By the eleventh day out to sea, my sea-sickness was so unrelenting I thought it would be a miracle if I would not have to be carried off that "boat," barely alive.

One incident took our minds off ourselves, at least for a few minutes. While we were lining up to be fed, out of the thick fog the glimmer of bright lights approached the Santa Paula at high speed. Thinking it might be a German surface raider, the ship's captain ordered all sirens and bells to be sounded, sending his crewmen scurrying to their lifeboat stations and loudspeakers ordered everyone on board to put on their "Mae Wests" (life jackets).

Within a few minutes it turned out that we had narrowly missed colliding with a brightly lighted hospital ship. I asked "V.D." if he could use his influence to get me transferred to that hospital ship. His reply: "Lose one of my 'germs?' Not on your life!"

On about the twelfth day we noticed the ship veered to the north, and three days later, we rushed up to the deck to see sheep grazing on the green hillsides of the Bristol Channel, a prettier sight to me than any painting I had ever seen. It was evening when we finally docked at Avonmouth, a port near Bristol. By this time I was so weak from my seasickness and lack of nourishment, Sgt. "V.D." had me carried up from the hold and added my barracks bag, field pack and helmet to his own gear as he guided me down the gangplank. As we disembarked, a British Army ATS (women's) band whose base drummer was ensheathed in a leopard skin greeted us with lively march music at midnight. Our G.I.'s, having seen little if any femininity for the past two weeks, responded with wolf whistles and "hubba hubba" catcalls, not a very gracious or gentlemanly show of appreciation, if anyone would have asked me at the time, which, of course, they didn't.

We had no clue as to our destination as we boarded a troop train whose compartment windows were painted black. As six of us jammed into each carriage compartment, the train whistle, sounding like a nearby tea kettle, signalled our moving forward, and we were aware by the sound of the clicks in the tracks that we were gradually picking up speed. We could see nothing through the opaque windows. After several long hours our train stopped, and we were ordered to "fall out! On the double!" When we opened our carriage doors, we blinked at the bright daylight as if we had just come out of a coal mine into the light. We formed up our whole battalion on the platform of a small town's rail station. We glanced at a map on the station wall and by spotting a well-worn spot on the map, we could see our new home away from home was a small resort town on the English Channel, about halfway between London and Land's End. Our Battery Commander, Captain "Marblemouth" Brundage, announced, "This is Swanage, in the County of Dorset, but don't anyone of you ever let anyone back home know anything about where you are, except that you're *'somewhere in England.'* All mail will be censored, and it's a serious offense to tell anyone the location of our unit. . .

And a word to the wise: We'd better be the best behaved outfit in the U.K. or there'll be hell to pay. Across the channel, over in France, is the enemy, and this town is within range of their V-1 flying bombs, so that means that the blackout along the coast is total. You owe it to your own safety and the safety of the whole area to see that there are no light leaks at the billets we'll be occupying up on the cliff overlooking the channel. Any questions?"

Some wag among us yelled, "Yes, sir! When do we eat?"

~~~

18.
Wintering in Swanage

Swanage, during the winter of 1944 was my home away from home. My battalion, waiting for our artillery pieces to arrive from the U.S., had little in the way of training it could offer us before we were shipped to France. Weekend passes to London and nearby Bournmouth were liberally handed out, and weeknights were taken up with "pub crawling" in the little town of Swanage. The town was so well blacked-out that in order to find our way down the long hill to the pubs, it became an entirely tactile rather than a visual exercise, our right hand feeling the hedges and fences on the way down, and our left hand doing the same on the way up the hill to our billets.

"The coldest winter in fifty years," the pub landlord told us, "So cold that the beer is freezing in the taps." The steep dip in temperature coincided with a shortage of kindling wood to get the coal started in our little fireplaces. There was no such thing as central heating in Swanage, or in the whole United Kingdom for all we knew. We soon discovered that starting a fire with just a match and newspapers was an exercise in futility. With the overburdened ancient plumbing freezing regularly, we had to resort to consigning floorboards, stair railings, window sills to our little piles of coal. This eventually made running downstairs to reveille formation in the street almost as hazardous as facing the enemy across the Channel.

A British government inspector, appalled at the headlong deterioration of the little old boarding houses turned into U.S. billets, posted on our Headquarters bulletin board the following notice: "It has been observed that at the present rate of destruction of these premises, you will be obliged to spend the rest of your stay in Swanage in tents, if the destruction doesn't cease immediately. Be sensible and heed this warning."

Uncle Sam had not been an ideal renter.

A few days after our arrival, our battalion took its first hike into the countryside beyond Swanage. We were told we would see our first castle, some five miles north of Swanage. As we passed through an old stone cottage-lined road, at the prospect of seeing our first castle, we were filled with anticipation. Our first castle! At least we S-2 (Intelligence Section) boys seemed to feel appreciation for the historical significance of our surroundings, having had some high school and college history behind us. We arrived at the site of Corfe Castle, a ruined relic of England's Civil War in the seventeenth century. A dense ground fog all but obliterated the Castle, except for a large sign at its base announcing that it was Corfe Castle. As we started our hike back to Swanage, the mists cleared enough for us to make out the faint outlines of a ruined tower and crumbling adjoining battlements. There was a romantic aura to the scene, a sort of visual metaphor of the violence that took place centuries past.

Imagine my excitement and impatience when I discovered that the Druid monuments of Stonehenge, a big panoramic photo of which had hung over my old eighth grade homeroom blackboard back in Oshkosh, was only a short distance (by American standards) from Swanage.

Those enigmatic stones gave me one of my earliest inklings that there was more to see and experience outside

Oshkosh, with the exception, of course of Chicago's World's Fair of 1933. I'll always remember the thrill of walking down the cobblestone streets of a transplanted Belgian Village, my father's enthusiasm for a fan dancer named Sally Rand, which became a main topic of conversation around his poker table, rivalled only by the new film "Ecstasy," starring Heddy Lamar.

One cold, clear morning I got off the bus on a two-lane highway near Amesbury and walked out to the unfenced meadow on which stood the mysterious Druid monuments. I was the only person there, at what I had always expected to be a place crowded with visitors. I recalled my little pre-enlistment prayer that I be sent to Europe, and having been taught from infancy that " gratitude is prayer," I knelt at the base of one of the upright stones. My forehead touched the rough, cold surface, and I thanked God for allowing me the chance to see and touch those stones, so full of mystery and wonder.

My Mentor, V.D.

My little billet, somewhat grandly named the Albany Court Hotel, had rooms on the second floor that accommodated in each room two to four soldiers and their equipment. I shared a room overlooking the Channel with my S-2 Section Sergeant Vincent De Ciucis, who endured the rest of the battalion's reference to his section as "V.D. and his germs." He was a soft-spoken, easy-going New Yorker with a thoughtful, philosophical view on life, war and destiny. His Italian relatives back home saw to it that he received every week a food package of salami, pasta and and pasta sauce. Our little fireplace became our kitchen stove, and every weekend he cooked spaghetti and taught me how to tell if the spaghetti was cooked "al dente": he would toss a fistful of the strands against the wallpaper, and if they didn't stick to the wallpaper, they were ready to eat. Out of our window we could look over the Channel toward our enemy over in France, less than fifty miles away. R.A.F. Typhoon fighter planes used the Channel near Swanage to practice gunnery at moving targets, and occasionally would encounter German "Doodlebugs" (V-1 rocket bombs on their way to Britain. They would shoot them down, or brazenly tilt the little wings of the rockets with their own wings, sending them back to France.

Our Outspoken Mascot

Little Albert, as we called him, for he wasn't more than three feet tall, was a Cockney boy who had been evacuated from London with his mother during the Blitz. They lived in a modest boarding house down the street from our even more modest billets. He lost no time in endearing himself as a kind of mascot for our battalion by showing up every morning to witness our six a.m. reveille formation, and by teaching us several stanzas of a ribald Cockney song, "Yankee Soldier."

One night, as Albert waited up for his mother to return home from a night of "pub crawling" with our Battalion Sergeant Major, he must not have appreciated what he saw through a crack in the front door where he lived. The next morning, as the battalion lined up in front of our billet for roll-call at reveille, Little Albert's little figure marched up to our battalion commander, who was taking the report, "All present and accounted for, sir!" from the sergeant major. Little Albert, tugging at our colonel's trench coat, with a squeaky voice for all the world to hear, pointed at the Sergeant Major and yelled, "Thar's the bloke wot pruned me maw!"

No simultaneous translation from Cockney to American English was needed to grasp the essential meaning of his complaint. The entire battalion broke into uncontrollable laughter and hoots at a crimson-faced sergeant major, who vainly tried to quiet down the whole battalion by shouting the command "Parade Rest!," which meant no talking; but as it turned out, it wasn't interpreted as meaning no laughing. Our stone-faced Captain Marble-mouth Brundage cracked a smile. Even the colonel, his face as crimson as the sergeant major's, couldn't put an end to the mass laughter and chortling.

V.D.'s "Germs"

Twelve college kids, by dint of their relatively high I.Q. scores were selected to man Captain Nelson's Intelligence (S-2) Section. Our Section Sergeant, Vincent DeCiucis, a balding, older man (he must have been at least thirty), a former short-hand reporter for the City of New York's judicial branch, was like a young father to us "Whiz Kids," as we were called by the rest of the battalion. The entire S-2 Section tended to keep to themselves, not out of a feeling of superiority, but by an all too evident reverse snobbery by the rest of the battalion, who manned the trucks and the artillery pieces, and regarded us as socially unacceptable. There was also the taint of anti-Semitism, for a majority of the S-2 Section was Jewish, and for some reason better-educated than the rest.

One evening at our headquarters billet, Mintern Manor, as we were watching a song-and-dance film, the light of the projector went out, leaving us all in total darkness. When the room's lights were suddenly turned on, to the shock and dismay of the Colonel and his staff, and to our collective amazement, two of our highest ranking master sergeants were discovered embracing each other. Within a few days, both were gone and never seen or heard from again.

Bucking for a "Section Eight"

As our turn to join in combat with the enemy approached, we had our share of characters who were "Bucking for a Section Eight," which in army jargon meant trying to get a discharge by reason of insanity. Only one in our battalion succeeded, a private first class from Brooklyn, who somehow convinced army psychiatrists that he was not fit to wear the uniform by repeatedly fishing for a whale in a bucket. A month after he was discharged and sent home, after we had arrived in France, a postcard from our "Battalion Nut" was posted on our Headquarter's bulletin board. It read, "You thought I was crazy, didn't you? Well, look at who's here and who's over there. Who's crazy now?

Mr. Gruber!"

~~~

19.
An "Outsider" in Our Midst

Back in the summer of 1935 an "outsider," certainly by Oshkosh standards, moved into a modest frame house two doors down the street from my modest frame house. He spoke a strange-sounding kind of English. To a ten-year-old Oshkosh ear what should have sounded like *nooze* came out more like *news*, and *duty* in his language meant *doody* in mine. But he was such a kindly, friendly old man I never held it against him that he mispronounced so many words.

Mr. Exworthy had been blind for many years. A talkative, cheerful man in his sixties, to me he was very old and very wise. Whenever I passed by his front porch, I would see him seated in an old weather-beaten rattan chair, reading bulky tomes of braille with his fingers. I looked forward to listening to him relate with those crisp consonants and round vowels, his memories of "a curious place inhabited for two thousand years by a race of the fiercest, the gentlest, the proudest, the humblest people on the face of the earth." They lived, he said, millions of them, in a huge city of some seven hundred square miles, with the ponderous-sounding name of London.

My new friend's rambling accounts of the London of Dickens and Queen Victoria made me a willing captive when I should have been doing my homework, especially especially in my weakest subjects: math, science, social studies, music, penmanship and manual training. His descriptions of the rogues and heroes of London's past were conveyed with a vividness, now that I look back on it, that only a no-longer sighted person could muster.

Nine years later the London of Queen Victoria, Dickens and Mr. Exworthy was to become an invariable destination during weekend passes from my artillery unit in Dorsetshire, on England's south coast. I was drawn to "The City," a warren of narrow streets covering three square miles, which from Dickens' time had become the world's greatest center of finance and commerce. By then I had come to the conclusion that Oshkosh was no longer the epicenter of my universe.

Few buildings within London's "City" had reached the year 1944 unscathed by Germany's aerial blitz. The area around St. Paul's Cathedral by night had a nightmarish, surrealistic aspect. Jagged, twisted walls became grotesque silhouettes by moonlight. Some streets were made inaccessible by barriers set up to keep out the curious and scavengers – not an ideal locale for a literary pilgrimage.

By the time of my visits to The City in 1944, the Royal Air Force's spirited defense had broken the back of the Luftwaffe. The job of clearing away vast expanses of rubble was just beginning to show results. The battered metropolis was still receiving sudden death and destruction from the sky by a new and daunting genre of weapons, the V-1 and V-2 flying bombs. More than two thousand of those rocket-propelled missiles rained down on Britain, most landing in the Greater London area. Hitler's latest development, the V-2, struck with no warning, taking not much more than three minutes to reach London from its launching sites on the continent.

One Sunday morning in June, 1944, hundreds of soldiers were attending services at the Guards' Chapel near

Buckingham Palace. A V-2 demolished the chapel and took its entire congregation. By this time, the Londoner, inclined to be fatalistic, could face tragic incidents such as this with stoic nonchalance. A police constable near Leicester Square told me, "One went to work, to the green grocer, to the cinema. Perhaps one would return home. Perhaps not."

On my frequent wartime visits to London, there was always the possibility that my sleep might be interrupted by a direct hit or a near-miss by a V-2. One Sunday morning I was lying on my cot in a Red Cross hostel in London's West End when a loud thunderclap of an explosion shook the building so violently that a pitcher of water standing on a fireplace mantle a few feet away crashed to the floor, and an enormous wind sucked makeshift cardboard window coverings out onto the street below. Later that morning I found out that a V-2 had landed a quarter of a mile away on the grounds of the Royal Chelsea Hospital, a home for old veterans.

Londoners told me that out of the immense dislocations, the shortages and ever-present danger, they had become kinder, more patient, and more helpful to one another. The ingrained, petty antagonisms of one class toward another were set aside, perhaps forever, to get on with the job of surviving and winning. I saw for myself the great supply of goodwill and mutual respect that was being built up during those bleak days.

My weekend passes to London ended abruptly when my unit was sent to France during the winter of 1944. My hasty visits to London had provided only a superficial acquaintance with the people of London. During those During those days they seemed preoccupied, shadowy and elusive.

At war's end in Europe, my unit pulled out of Czechoslovakia, was sent back to the U.K. and disbanded. As if in another incarnation, I found myself back in London, this time as an army criminal investigations agent. This time, my daily work brought the people of London into sharp focus. For the first time I was becoming aware of all the contradictory attributes and qualities my old blind friend had so often mentioned.

To make generalizations about such a cosmopolitan conglomeration of human beings carries certain risks: contradiction and ridicule, especially for an outsider. But somehow I don't feel overly foolhardy in offering the following observations: The Londoner, whether native-born, a black man from Jamaica or a refugee from Poland, every Londoner is aware of a special quality they all share: a distillation of twenty centuries of history and an accumulation of experience deposited by successive waves of invaders and immigrants. Londoners are aware of a thicker veneer of civilization than enjoyed by many of their contemporaries on the continent of Europe. Londoners may be perceived to exhibit a certain smugness on this score. Even among the bizarrely coiffed and dressed youths in London's King's Road an innate sense of individual worth and a deep-seated desire for respectability, an underlying warmth, are there, waiting to be tapped. What is more quickly discerned is a sense of humor, an inner serenity, along with a disarming shyness, all of which make life in a crowded urban environment tolerable, even enjoyable.

One evening, just after the end of the war with Japan, the London Provost Marshal's Office sent me to interview a Lady Wadia. She lived in an elegant flat in Green Street, in London's fashionable West End. She had put in a claim against the United States government for one hundred guineas as compensation for the ruining of her green-sequinned evening gown. Overly exuberant G.I. victory celebrants had dumped a pail of water, pail and all, on her as she and her husband walked past an American Army billet. They were returning to their flat after an evening at the theatre.

When I called on Lady Wadia, a winsome, middle-aged woman, she offered me tea and biscuits. Her maid brought in her tattered gown, and Lady Wadia related the incident to me with a lightness and good humor that belied the fact that she had barely escaped serious injury from the prank. When I asked for a description of the offending soldiers, assuring her that they would be arrested and prosecuted, she demurred gently, saying,

"Never mind. After all, your chaps are far from home."

I was to hear similar refrains many times in the course of my work in London. It often occurred to me that I couldn't be certain that New Yorkers, Chicagoans, or Los Angelenos would be as tolerant and forgiving if they had experienced similar excesses by British soldiers "away from home."

A quarter of a century later, this time completely free of any gravitational pull from Oshkosh, I roamed about London, this time as a photographer. The great city was undergoing many architectural face lifts, not all for the better. Huge monoliths of steel and glass, distressingly similar to those of New York, Chicago and Los Angeles were making surviving old landmarks even more precious and appreciated. Londoners, though emotionally and intellectually devoted to their city's past, were resignedly witnessing the de-Londonization process as an inevitable concomitant of what many call "progress."

An "Outsider" in Our Midst

A smiling, bemedalled Commissionaire doorman at the entrance of an airline office greets my wife with a cheery "God Bless." A bus conductress, busily making change for a passenger, takes time to say, "Mind the step, luv." A Bobby in front of the Guildhall relates with touches of eloquence what will take place when the Lord Mayor arrives in his carriage and is ceremonially escorted inside. His words are tinged with pride and enthusiasm. A Queen's Horseguard, still as a statue at his guard post at Whitehall sneaks a wink to a throng of Japanese tourists festooned with cameras. A Sunday fisherman sits in a heavy downpour, shielded by an umbrella along the bank of Hyde Park's Serpentine, as quiet, tranquil and patient as the water at his feet. A husky worker, climbing to his high perch atop a construction crane, stops to admire the panorama of his great city below. A bevy of uniformed school girls giggle and applaud as a troop of young soldiers marches past their school yard. The soldiers pretend not to notice. A "cabby" nods deferentially and tips his cap as his passengers alight from his immaculate old taxi. These are Londoners.

~~~

20.

A New Expertise

In the winter of 1944 as we crossed the Belgian border and entered the embattled Third Reich, we had little sense of direction, other than Germany always was to the east, even though our compasses insisted we were travelling in a more southerly direction. We were a two-man team, travelling alone in a jeep, towing a small trailer crammed with a radio, a generator, and all our earthly possessions.

Soon after our troops had landed on the French beaches on D-Day, the Germans became aware that our jeeps had windshields folded down against the hood and covered with burlap to create no glare to attract their attention. This gave them the lethal opportunity to string almost invisible piano wire from one tree to another across roads, at throat height. By the time our battalion landed in France, this nasty trick was foiled by having a six-foot tall angle-iron bar topped by a cutter bar welded to the bumper of every jeep.

As our two-man o.p. (observation post) travelled down dark, forested roads, there was always the possibility that a sniper would try to pick us off from up in a tree; the only comforting thought being that if he missed, we could return fire to keep him concealed while we increased the distance between us. Then there was the ever-present chance of hitting a mine if we carelessly wandered off the macadam onto the soft shoulder of the road. Tree busts from the enemy's 88 mm. artillery shells, another nervosity, would send a hail of shrapnel straight down, so a foxhole was of little protection. Since an o.p. acted as the eyes of our artillery, we had a high priority on the enemy's "wanted" list. When setting up our o.p., the first thing we had to do was to dig a hole deep enough to "bury" our radio generator, powered by a gasoline engine. This had to be done to muffle the sound of the engine, which, noisy, could give away our position. So, all in all, we were engaged in a profession which could be considered hazardous to our health.

We were issued British "Cardex" encoding devices which we used to encode our map coordinates of our o.p. so that the Germans, if they intercepted our radio reports back to our c.p., would have to try to decode our message. By the time they got it decoded, we would already have moved on to another location.

We rather enjoyed the "cat and mouse" aspect of our daily life. Careful camouflage of both sight and sound was our best life insurance policy. Smoking, for us, would have been lethal, fifty years before our government announced that nicotine was a killer.

Before we landed in France, I had the dubious honor to have been selected to attend the British Army's Southern District Headquarters Mine and Booby Trap School, near Nether Wallop, situated in a cow pasture dotted with Nissen huts on the Salisbury Plain. British Army mine experts conducted the training, which was realistic and thorough. On "graduation night" we had to crawl down a narrow lane marked with pennants bearing a skull and crossbones in black on a yellow background, and "feel" with prods mines that were buried a foot deep; then, oh, then, oh, so carefully remove the detonator on top of the mine. If we made a mistake, the mine, a dummy, wouldn't blow up, but in the adjacent lane a small charge of T.N.T. would go off, sending bits of shale and sand flying through the air. On my first try,

I caused a charge to go off which not only startled me but earned a good tongue-lashing from my instructor.

Since we arrived on the continent, I was to put my newly acquired expertise to use within a few days of our arrival. We were bivouacked one night in a staging area outside Soissons in Normandy. Walking along the perimeter of our motor pool, I found a crate filled with German push-pull mine detonators. The detonators are the part that is screwed into the top of the mine, and sets off a small explosive cap which detonates the mine if it's stepped on or if a trip-wire is pulled. Delighted with my find as a philatelist would be with a new, rare stamp to add to his collection, I carried the crate full of detonators into the command post tent where our First Sergeant was working on his morning report.

"Look, Sarge, look what I just found!" I announced, "German push-pull mine detonators!"

First Sergeant Farish Helton, as if sudden death were staring him in the face, panic-stricken, shouted, "Git them infernal thangs otta hyah! Walk, don't run with them thangs! If yore still 'live after gitten ridda them, I'll be waitin fo' you to report fo' extry guard duty!"

It was then that I learned a little knowledge could be a dangerous thing.

~~~

21.

Two Nights in Belgium

It was in December, 1944 when our unit pulled into the courtyard of a small château, in Verviers, which our colonel had decided would make a fine command post, possibly possessing a few bottles of wine or beer in its cellar. What we found instead was a former couturier school, built in the style of a seventeenth century Versailles château, recently vacated by the retreating Germans. They left the place in a shambles, with piles of rubbish spread over the parquet floors, and ashes of burned documents in the fireplaces.

Our colonel had me drive him across town to what appeared to be the town's best hotel, a shabby, down-at-the-heals looking establishment bearing the overly proud name of Grand Hotel. As we entered the narrow entrance hall, to our left on the wall behind glass was a mural of Belgian women making lace. Their bleary-eyed expressions reminded me of a W.P.A. mural in my old elementary school's lobby, back in Oshkosh. That mural's students and teachers all had those same bleary eyes. I carried the colonel's bedroll up to what the concièrge had assured him was the best room in the hotel, dinky by our American motel standards, and dingy by any standard. An antique-looking wooden-framed telephone with a hand crank hung on the wall. While I was unpacking the colonel's gear, bright flashes and the rumble of artillery reminded us that there was a war going on, and nearby, too.

One warm summer night some twenty-five years later, my wife and I drove into the same Belgian town, Verviers, and spent the night in the same old Grand Hotel, and in the same room Colonel Brannan had occupied. The whole experience had an eery déjà-vue quality: The hotel hadn't changed a bit: the same mural in the entrance hall, the same old hand-crank telephone on the wall. But beyond all that, during the night a fierce electrical storm awoke us, and the distant thunder and lightening flashes brought back as if it had been that night years before, my wartime night in Verviers.

The next morning I took my wife over to see the château, where I had been billeted during the Battle of the Bulge. Instead of a small château, there stood in its place a modern, functional building of several floors. Surprised and disappointed, we entered the building and I asked the receptionist, "What happened to the Couturier School?"

The woman, too young to have been aware of the building's predecessor, called the directress of the school to the reception desk. The older woman, amused as if a Rip van Winkle had just come back out of the past, said,

"Oh, monsieur, didn't you know that in December, 1944 the Germans levelled the old château with their artillery? You must have left just before it happened!"

~~~

22.

The Ides of March

The war years for many were years the locusts had eaten, never to be restored. With all its horrors and tedium, the war for me meant liberation from what seemed to me a stultifying existence in Oshkosh. It meant escape, adventure, excitement, close calls. The Army was a good provider.

In the winter and spring of 1944-45 I was an air-ground combat intelligence observer with an anti-aircraft battalion. We had trained and practiced our art in southern England, crossed over to France, pushed into Belgium, were thrown back by a massive German counter-attack, then came back through Belgium and into Germany. We were a tiny cog, my battalion, in a well-oiled killing machine, the U.S. Third Army, that was tearing into the heart of a tottering Third Reich.

There were times, sad to say, that our Third Army was not as well-oiled as it could have been, thanks to a breed of G.I. entrepreneurs who would have made J. Pierpont Morgan envious. They were diverting whole shipments of P.O.L. (petroleum products) to a burgeoning black market back in France. Many members of a so-called "millionaire railroad battalion" were court-marshalled and sent to the jungles of New Guinea as infantrymen to redeem themselves. These "entrepreneurs" caused recurring shortages of fuel for our trucks and tanks, fuel badly needed to keep up our forward momentum into Germany.

During one of these enforced halts, we spent several days waiting for fuel supplies at a pretty resort town on the west bank of the Rhine, Bad Godesberg. One cold March morning at four o'clock we were awakened and told to report to Captain Nelson, our unit's intelligence officer. Steve Kwasny and I were given a new map, showing the location of our next observation post, across the river, and up the Autobahn (super highway) about fifteen miles to the north. Under cover of darkness we were to set up our o.p. on a hillside overlooking enemy-held territory.

About five miles south of our newly assigned position, a hail of machine gun bullets interspersed with tracers whizzed over our jeep and trailer. They were so low, that if we hadn't folded our windshield over the jeep's hood, the bullets would have smashed the glass into our faces. The folded-down windshield was a precaution we had been ordered to take, not one we would have preferred, due to the cold wind blowing in our faces, but it made sense to keep the windshield down and covered with burlap so as not to reflect light and attract the enemy's attention. Be that as it may, something attracted their attention, and probably thinking we were the point of an attack or an enemy patrol, they began shooting up into the sky a series of parachute flares. Fortunately for us, a moonless night and thick ground fog made their marksmanship inaccurate. Steve, at the wheel, turned the jeep into a grassy median strip in an effort to high-tail it back to the c.p.. All the while, machine gun bullets were flying just over our heads. Once in the median strip, our jeep's wheels got bogged down in the mud. Steve was frantically fighting a stubborn four-wheel drive gear shift to try to extricate us. Meanwhile the wheels were spinning around, lowering us deeper into the mud. This was making us a lower target, which was lucky for us, since the bullets kept getting closer to our heads. The tires finally struck some rocks in the mud, and we were able to force the jeep through the rest of the median strip and out onto the south-bound lane of the Autobahn, to safety.

A couple of days later, the enemy having been cleared out of the area north of us, as our whole battalion traveled north on the Autobahn in broad daylight, Steve and I in our jeep passed the very spot where we had been bogged down in the mud. We saw our deep tire tracks, and we saw something more: the tire tracks were deep into an area marked with black and yellow skull and crossbone pennants. We had driven through the middle of a mine field and had come out on the other side completely unscathed! My mother's prayers had not gone unanswered.

We were all caught up in a collective, almost insane hatred of the enemy. It was difficult to regard them as human beings, mothers' sons, children's fathers. What we saw in factory yards how they treated their slave laborers, how they had looted most of western Europe and committed such atrocious mass-killings left us with no sympathy for the retribution they were now receiving. It was also a matter for us of kill or be killed. During those days I would have been happy to see every last one of them wiped off the face of the earth. When we saw German corpses, we would say to ourselves, "One less kraut to infect the world," so filled we were with the contagion of hatred for the Germans. Notwithstanding having grown up in a predominantly German community, I put out of my mind and conscience the kindness of Laura, our German-born nursemaid, the strong, unequivocal indoctrination of moral absolutes instilled in us by our teachers, many of whom had German names, and our warm, loving German-speaking neighbors who were always there when needed. But after seeing day after day the destruction and suffering the Germans left in their wake, I was easily caught up in the mass insanity and desire for vengeance.

Something was to happen that was to change my thinking, that all Germans are brutes. One morning, near Siegen, I was left alone at our o.p. while Steve went back to the c.p. for supplies. The sector had been recently cleared of the enemy, and was quiet. I was standing in an abandoned German searchlight position on a gentle slope overlooking a meadow. Down in the meadow, about a hundred yards from the o.p., an old man was starting his spring plowing, even though there were still patches of snow on the ground. His horse looked better fed than he did.

As I stood there looking over a parapet, scanning the road below, an American weapons carrier loaded with G.I.'s approached my position. The farmer, being closer to the weapons carrier, could see them unlimbering their weapons and aiming at me! He looked up at me and began to wave frantically. I instinctively reacted by ducking down behind the parapet, just as a fusillade of Schmeisser "burp gun" bullets whistled inches over my head. For once, I was thankful for my short stature.

That farmer, a German, had saved my life! He let me live to kill more Germans! As the weapons carrier raced down the road away from my position, I emptied my full clip of eight rounds at them. I couldn't tell if I hit any of them or not.

The farmer left his plow and walked up to the parapet. He smiled a toothless smile and pointed to where my would-be assailants had passed by and said,

"Nicht Amerikaner. Deutschen!"

The farmer went back to his plowing before I could muster any words of thanks in German. A few minutes later Steve drove up to the position. "I heard firing around here. What's going on?"

"I got sprayed over my head by a bunch of Germans wearing American helmets who were tearing down the road in one of our weapons carriers. They had Schmeisser machine pistols. If it hadn't been for that farmer down there, who signalled me to duck, I would have been hit! They were drawing a bead on *me* when *he* spotted what they were doing!"

"Christ, John, I just passed that truck! They were going like a bat outta hell!"

Steve brought fresh C-rations, little olive-drab cans full of mushy spaghetti and tiny meatballs, a new map of the area we were going to the next day, and a message marked "Urgent!" It warned all units in that sector of German infiltrators wearing G.I. uniforms, cutting our telephone lines and laying mines on the roads.

As we sat down for our evening meal, the old farmer, with a young boy in tow, approached our position. He was carrying a bottle of wine. It was hard for me to get the words out. I knew enough in German to say "thanks," but that seemed so inadequate. He seemed to appreciate the language barrier between us, and after hearing my "Vielen dank" he uncorked the bottle, offering it to me first. Steve's distrust for the Germans came to the fore, and pointing to the old man's grandson, poured some wine into his canteen cup and handed it to the boy. The boy looked at his grandfather, who was smiling and nodding in agreement. After the boy had taken a hearty swig, we then all drained the bottle of its sweet Rhine wine. I wished then and now that I could have said in German, "I owe you my life," but all I could do was to give him our two-day supply of K- and C-rations. I think our generosity touched him. He left us, genially saluting us all the way down to his house.

~~~

23.

Getting "Busted"

One night, at Bad Godesburg, just before we crossed the Rhine, my ascent up the military ladder took a sudden nose-dive. Corporal Kwasny and I had just arrived at our battalion command post from our previous observation post position to be reassigned to a new location, and to pick up new maps of the area on the east side of the river. We were told to move out the next morning, at four, under the cover of darkness. That meant we had to get some sleep somewhere at the c.p.. Sgt. Deciucis told me that since we were the last o.p. to report in, all the rooms of the first floor were already taken. We would have to take our bedrolls up to the attic and settle in there for the rest of the night. During the past several nights we had heard the swooshing sound of German ME 262 jet fighters, and an occasional burst of machine gun fire from these "Bed-check Charlies," as we called them, sending us a strong signal that their strafing of the rooftops meant they knew their enemy was in the area, and they intended to make us feel unwelcome.

Since we had roomed together back in England, my S-2 (Intelligence Section) sergeant and I were on cordial, first-name terms. I never felt the least bit intimidated by our easy-going sergeant's higher rank. Sergeant Deciucis reiterated, "John, there's just no more room for you and you and Kwasny downstairs. There's only the attic."

I was appalled at the idea of being a tempting target for an ME 262, and protested, "Like hell, Vincent! You're out of your mind if you think I'm going to let a bed-check Charlie strafe me! To hell with that!"

My friend, I could tell by his expression, was feeling the logic behind my outburst, and I was sure he was about to figure out a safer alternative for me. But I didn't realize that within earshot of us was our battery commander, Captain "Marblemouth" Brundage, a stickler for military courtesy. He had heard me sounding off to my sergeant, and he wasn't about to let it go unpunished. His hands on his hips, like a king about to take a knighthood away from one of his vassals, he loftily announced, "Private First Class Livingstone, for your insubordination, you are hereby demoted to the grade of Private."

I stood there, stunned by his edict, not able to reply except for a grief-laden "Yes, Sir!" I saluted, made an about face, and marched out of the room, my military career in tatters. Sergeant Deciucis, as dismayed as I was, told me later that night, "This is the Army, John, not a fraternity house."

Kwasny and I noticed a nearby cemetery and bedded down among the protective tombstones.

What was most galling was the fact, well broadcast throughout the battalion, that there was now for the first time, one man who was outranked by even the newest private first class in the Third Army, and his name was Private Livingstone.

How could I keep the awful truth from my parents? I could no longer write my slightly more exalted rank of Pfc on the return address part of my V-mail letters to them. When first Sergeant Helton heard about my demotion, he woke me up and patting me on the shoulder, said, "Private Livin'stun! Now thet sounds reel nice! You prob'ly don't reelize it, but a soldier cain't call hisself a reel soldier 'less he's been busted at least once't and gotten a dose of clap."

I decided not to share with my parents that little dissertation of commiseration. Instead, knowing that "Marblemouth" Brundage was also our unit censor, I would write a tear-jerker account of what and how it happened, telling them all the extenuating circumstances behind my demotion, stressing it wasn't the big reduction of $6.50 a month in my pay that saddened me, but that I , who had volunteered at the age of seventeen, had always served my country to the best of my ability, and had looked forward to a career I could be proud of. Beyond my letter, I was determined to regain my Pfc stripe as soon as possible. Whenever I got back to the c.p., I would mope around the sergeant major's desk, bemoaning my lowly status, and I being the unit's mine and booby trap expert! Col. Brannan, who always had a soft spot in his heart for me (he always called me "Livin'stone, ole man") would be bound to know about my new lowly status, and might do something about it.

My second cousin, Morton Lee, offered to remove my single stripe from my uniform "free of charge," but in the next breath half-jokingly "pulled his rank" on me, ordering me to "Polish my boots, Private!"

The following payday, I was thrilled to receive the same pay as I always received. Captain Brundage had not gotten around to letting me know that my rank of Pfc had been reinstated.

Now I could *almost* call myself a *real soldier*.

~~~

24.

"Kristalnacht"
*(Crystal Night)**

It was a cold, windy night in March. Our command
post had just been moved into an old mansion on the
outskirts of Cologne. Our battalion commander had not
been seen since our arrival there, and for good reason. He
was up in the attic, wrapping and packing for shipment, back
to his home in Georgia, crystal goblets and tumblers. I was
sent up to the attic to help him with his new acquisitions.

"Livin'stone, ole man," he drawled, "I'll wrap and
you hammer down those crates so's nothin' falls out."

I recalled how one Sunday morning back in Camp
Stewart, Georgia when I was on K.P. duty, he noticed how I
was struggling to build a mop rack. My colonel, dressed in
his class "A" uniform and heading for the parking lot where
his wife was waiting for him, went back to the barracks and
put on his fatigue uniform. He made his wife wait for the
better part of an hour while he helped me construct that mop
rack. There must have been serious repercussions when he
got back to his car.

Now, a year later, in the territory of an enemy that
had been looting most of Europe for the past five years, it
didn't pique my conscience to be an accessory to the semi-
crime of "liberating" German goods in a house that probably
belonged to one of the town's biggest Nazis. Besides, I

figured, I could make it up to him for all the trouble I must have caused him that Sunday back in Camp Stewart.

While the colonel was wrapping the crystal, the air over the roof was shattered with a loud tearing sound, much like the sound of a window shade being ripped in half.

"Damn! Those kraut 88 shells are coming in right over the roof! Git your helmet on and let's git down to the basement!" The colonel was shouting and cursing, as we rushed downstairs, and he shook his fist in the enemy's direction, shouting, "Don't you dare crack any of *mah crystal*, damn you!"

The shelling lasted for several more minutes. Then it was silenced by what must have been our effective counter-fire.

We never stayed longer in one location than three days, as we pressed deeper into the Third Reich. During a day's halt in the town of Wetzlar, my buddies and I were able to walk through a relatively undamaged part of the Leitz Optical Company's lens assembly department. I always had a special reverence for the Leica camera, the most precision-made and highest-priced camera in the world. There was a drugstore back in Oshkosh that catered to the "Carriage trade," Coe's Drugstore on Main Street. Before the war they proudly displayed on a red velvet background in their camera counter a gleaming Leica camera, bearing a price tag of $250.00. Owning a precious Leica in those depression days was only for the town's one or two remaining millionaires.

Now, as I stood in the home of the Leica camera, I saw hanging on the far wall one of those ubiquitous photos under glass that we had been seeing everywhere we went in Germany, a portrait of Der Führer. On a high wooden workbench in front of us stood a pile of partially assembled

Leica lenses. We all picked up the lenses and hurled them with all our strength at the portrait, smashing the glass and Hitler's physiognomy beyond recognition. It was a kind of catharsis, venting some of our hatred on an image of a devil incarnate.

Fifty years later, a friend who owned a camera shop in Carmel told me that he was going to visit the Leitz factory at Wetzlar within a few weeks. I related to him the "Kristalnacht" we had inflicted on the Leitz Company back in 1945. Would he be telling his hosts about it?

"Some things are better left unsaid," he answered.

~~~

*(Footnote: "Kristalnacht": on nights in pre-war Germany gangs of Nazi thugs rampaged through German towns and cities, smashing Jewish-owned shop windows and looting them of their contents while the police looked on approvingly.)

25.

The Late Tom Gabriel

Tom Gabriel and I met during our summer semester in 1943 at the University of Wisconsin. He was just my age, and like me, wasn't particularly looking forward to the possibility of being drafted into the Navy. His eyes lighted up when I explained to him how I was going to "beat the draft" by enlisting in the Army's Enlisted Reserve, to be called to active duty after my eighteenth birthday.

"That makes a lot of sense, John, but I don't know that my mom and dad will buy the idea," he said.

"Look, Tom. You live in Appleton, just a half hour's drive from Oshkosh. Why don't you get your parents to come down some Sunday to meet my folks? They'll convince them that it's the right thing to do." I knew that my dad especially was "sold" on the idea, and saw all the advantages for me.

Tom and his parents came to lunch the following weekend, and both sets of parents hit it off well. Tom's dad, like mine, was a self-made, self-educated successful businessman, deeply concerned about his son's future. By the end of the day, it was decided that Tom would enlist along with me the following week, such was the urgency we all felt.

One afternoon Tom and I happened to pass by the music listening room in the university's Memorial Union student center, and heard the melodic strains of *"Capricio*

Espangnole. " "Catchy toon, ain't it?" I said, trying to sound cute.

"Shore is!" Tom rejoined.

During our weekly hour of billiards down in the University's Ratskeller, both of us, smitten by the catchy melody, began humming it in two-part harmony. It did nothing to improve our game, but it set a sort of precedent: whenever we felt especially carefree, we would launch into our abridged duet version of *Capricio Espagnole.*

Shortly after our eighteenth birthdays Tom and I received identical orders to report to Fort Sheridan, Illinois for induction. What stands out in my mind about our first day in the Army was Tom's flippant answer to the processing sergeant when he asked him what religion to stamp on his "dog tags."

"Just put on a big fat "A" for atheist," Tom answered.

I wasn't impressed with his perverse sense of humor. "Come on, Tom! Your folks brought you up to be a Catholic, and they would really be upset to find that all they've done for you so that you could get some college education is being repaid by you declaring you're an atheist."

"Okay, Okay, you win. Sarge, put down a "C" on those tags," Tom decided.

One week before the war ended in Europe, our unit had set up observation posts near the Czech border, at Eger. Tom was about a mile down the line from my o.p., when I heard a burst of machine gun fire in the distance. This late in the war, it was beginning to be unusual to hear any gunfire at all. By this time, the enemy, thoroughly trounced, fearing far more capture by the Russians coming from the east, were surrendering in droves. That evening I went back to our C.P.

to get rations and a new location assignment for the o.p.. As I entered the S-2 section I saw Sgt. DeCiucis wiping away tears with his olive drab toilet paper.

"What's up, V.D.?" I asked.

Our S-2 sergeant was hardly audible. "It's Tom, Tom Gabriel. Well, he was hit today, his whole hip shot away by machine gun fire. He lingered for over six hours."

I asked myself, why of all people, Tom? To this day I still ask myself that same question.

"Did Tom receive Last Rites?" I was anxious to know.

Sergeant Deciucis, a devout Catholic, much to my and his relief replied, "Yes."

His parents, informed by War Department telegram, also received letters from Tom's battalion commander, his battery commander, Sergeant DeCuicis, and his best friend, me. It was the hardest thing I had ever had to do, writing that letter. If it hadn't been for me, Tom would probably still be alive. Now the thought of returning home, of having to face his parents filled me with dread.

Now, more than fifty years later, whenever I happen to hear those familiar strains of *Capricio Espagnole*, I think of Tom Gabriel, not with completely dry eyes.

~~~

26.
The Wehrmacht's Last Gasp

The war in Europe was in its last week. My battalion had by this time pushed into the border areas of Czechoslovakia's Sudetenland – "Pushed" is a bit too strong a way to put it; by then German resistance had all but crumbled. They knew the end was near, and their units, ill-fed and exhausted, were "going west," finding it infinitely preferable to surrender to the Americans and the British than to their avenging enemies from the east, the Soviet armies. They had a good idea what captivity in Russian hands would mean: starvation, brutal treatment, slavery conditions, long-delayed repatriation if they survived.

The Sudeten Germans who lived in the Czech border areas were already being evicted, sent to Germany in box cars, by the newly liberated Czech National Police.

As the Russian hordes were approaching, our formerly stubborn enemy was only too happy to call it quits and surrender to us, whole units at a time. By this time it wasn't unusual for small groups of German soldiers, worn out and hungry, to walk up to our positions, holding their hands above their heads, shouting "Kamerad!" We two on our observation post soon learned that if we didn't shoo them off, there would be more "waiting in the wings" to take advantage of our hospitality. This was proving to be a major distraction from our o.p. duties. We used stock phrases: *"Nicht heute! Morgen, vieleicht!"* (*Not today! Tomorrow, perhaps!*) We knew we were about to take Pilsen to the east within the next few days, and would meet the Russians there, leaving the Germans caught between us and the tender mercies of the Russians.

The gaunt, unshaven German soldiers, when they approached our o.p., reminded me of the depression days back in Oshkosh when hoboes would come to our back door, humbly asking for food or a little cash. If my mother would give them a handout, they would show their appreciation by marking with chalk a cross on the sidewalk in front of our house, signifying that their fellow "knights of the road" could expect a soft touch at 177 Central Avenue.

On an idyllic, quiet evening in early May, 1945 (by "quiet" meaning no nearby gunfire or drone of bombers overhead) I was sitting on a little stone bridge admiring the rural scenery and sniffing the spring air laden with the smell of lilacs, absolutely minding my own business, when a lone German officer walked out of the woods along the road ahead and in passable English said, "I want to surrender to a Major or higher offitzeer!" He was unarmed, and limping badly, so I made the mistake of replying, "Ja. O.K." I grabbed hold of my rifle and slipped my finger into the trigger guard and pushed forward the safety catch, just to make sure.

The officer slowly pulled out of his top tunic pocket a whistle and blew it three short times. All of a sudden, a huge crowd of soldiers, horses and wagons swarmed out of the woods on both sides of the road, and formed up in company-sized units. There were soldiers on the road as far as my eyes could see. These were no longer "elite" or battle-hardened soldiers, but the dregs of what remained of the once vaunted Wehrmacht, old men and young boys wearing filthy, ill-fitting uniforms, some without soles left in their boots. They were a regimental-sized unit of Hitler's "Volksturm" troops, who, in comparison with my old Wisconsin State Guard soldiers, made us look like West Pointers on parade.

My neighborhood clairvoyant, Mrs. LeDoyt's admonition to me before I went into the army came back in loud decibels: "Don't you go 'round stickin' your neck out. Don't be a coward, but don't be no hero, neither. Don't take any fool chances, and you'll come out just fine."

There I was, a lone skinny, nineteen-year-old kid, escorting the remnants of a whole regiment, some three thousand soldiers, to a nearby infantry command post. Many were sick with dysentery, and our long column inched forward at a snail's pace while many broke out of the formation to relieve themselves at the edge of the road.

As our pathetic-looking procession made its way to the command post, a field staff car bearing a general's two stars came up to me, and the general, seated in the back seat of the open car, called me over to him. "What the hell are you doing? Where are you going with that mob?" He demanded.

I saluted, and answered, "Private first Class Livingstone, sir, on an observation post of the 444th AAA Battalion. I was just sitting here alone, minding my own business, when a German Major came out of the woods to surrender. The next thing I knew he blew a whistle, and all those people came out of the woods onto the road. I'm escorting them to the nearest C.P., sir!"

The general, turning to a Lieutenant colonel sitting next to him, pointed at me, saying, "Get that kid's name and hometown newspaper, and give him a little write-up. Nothing heroic, just the facts." Then turning to me, he said.

"Well, son, you'll have something to tell your children and grandchildren someday, how you captured single-handed

112

a whole damn German regiment." He laughed, and ordered the driver to move on.

A few days later we met the Russians at Pilsen and held a joint victory ceremony in the city's main square. For us the war was over.

~~~

27.

Shoot-out in the Rue Réamur Corral

When you say "downtown" in Oshkosh, it means the business district along Main Street and a block or two on either side. *Downtown* in London or Paris would bring the response, "What on earth do you mean?" But when I wrote my parents to be on the lookout for an article in the May 13th, 1946 issue of *Life Magazine* entitled "Paris Gunplay" in *downtown* Paris, that had much more significance to them than to mention the arrondissement, or the name of the street, Rue Réamur.

The American penchant for creating and "solving" problems with guns in city streets, a heretofore unknown phenomenon in London and Paris, was becoming a commonplace occurrence, regularly reported by the foreign press. The presence of hordes of G.I.'s toting German souvenir pistols, and the number of executions for capital crimes taking place in the ETO after the end of the war in Europe was becoming an embarrassment to the War Department. Early in 1946 it was decreed that after a certain cut-off date, all executions would take place at Fort Dix, New Jersey.

One of the condemned G.I.'s, Private Eddie Jones from Cleveland, Ohio, convicted of murdering an Army courier, was awaiting transfer to Fort Dix when he feigned an attack of appendicitis at *Caserne Mortier*, renamed the Paris Detention Barracks. He overpowered a guard, disarmed him and put on his military police uniform. He then freed several other prisoners: Privates Lee, Blackburn, Pitlick and Jordan. In the shoot-out at the prison, Jordan was killed but the others escaped. For the next two weeks the military police and the C.I.D. responded to numerous tips, only to arrive too late, or to find the tips to be false leads.

One of the false tips sent me and several other agents rushing to meet a train from Rheims at Gare du Nord Station. As I entered one of the coaches, carrying a Thompson sub-machine gun, I chanced upon a friend of one of our agents, Flo Allen, a Rheims Red Cross Club director who had come to spend a weekend in Paris. It took some explaining to convince her we were not there to impress her in some way with the kind of work we were doing.

Then one morning in early May, I was walking toward La Grande Taverne, a large Army-run restaurant better described as a mess hall. I was salivating at the thought of a stainless steel tray overflowing with chunks of roast beef, mashed potatoes and gravy, and canned sliced peaches when a burst of gunfire echoed against the walls of tall buildings along the street. Eddie Jones and his pals, on the loose in Paris, recognized a French detective and opened fire on him. Within minutes the street was filled with American military police, C.I.D. men and chrome-helmeted French police, and the chase was on. Any further reverie about lunch evaporated as I drew my .45 automatic pistol from its shoulder holster and joined in the chase. During the mélée that followed, a French pedestrian was killed and a French *Agent de Police* was wounded. We finally ran our quarry to ground in the middle of the newspaper district, our achievement duly recorded by almost every newspaper photographer in Paris. *Life Magazine* got a good set of photos to run with their story, entitled "Paris Gunplay - Three G.I. Jail-breakers are Caught After Wild Chase in the Streets."

A Paris newspaper the following day carried a banner headline laced with sarcasm: *"Chicago Sur Seine."*

Whenever we raided brothels and cheap hotels in search of AWOLS and deserters, the French police, who always accompanied us, phobically and prudently chose not to enter the premises along with us. They remained in their cars until they knew there were no G.I.'s to contend with. They left that up to us, so paranoid were they of our G.I. gun-slingers.

> *(A month after returning home I received word that a nineteen-year-old French interpreter was killed on one of our raids on a brothel.)*

The article in *Life Magazine* made my parents and many other Americans back home aware for the first time that significant numbers of our G.I.'s were not exactly goodwill ambassadors, that our national propensity for gunplay not only happened in our movies.

Yankee entrepreneurial talent blossomed in the streets of Paris. No Army supply room was safe from being broken into and ransacked by lawless G.I.'s, eager to make a quick buck selling stolen clothing, blankets, food, cigarettes, gasoline, tires, vehicles to the flourishing French *"Marché Noir"* (black market). Gangs of AWOLS and deserters backed up stolen trucks to Army freight cars, broke the seals, and emptied their contents, delivering them to black market operators for instant cash. The French, so deprived of staples and luxury goods during the long years of German occupation, were buying anything the G.I.'s could lay their hands on, even such lowly commodities as ping pong balls and cigarette lighter flints. Army stockades in and around Paris were crammed with G.I. miscreants awaiting trial or serving sentences.

Private Eddie Jones, aboard a troopship bound for the U.S. and his ultimate execution, attacked a guard on board the ship and strangled him. If he had been executed in Paris, a life would have been saved.

It came as no surprise when my parents back in Oshkosh wrote me that they had seen the "tremendous coverage" of the gun battle in *Life*. My mother, as was her habit, closed her letter with "Jack dear, don't get into any fights over there."

~~~

March, 1945, Weiden, Germany: "dressing up" in Nazi uniforms. Our colonel ordered our sergeant to "take 'em out and shoot 'em." We survived the jocular order.

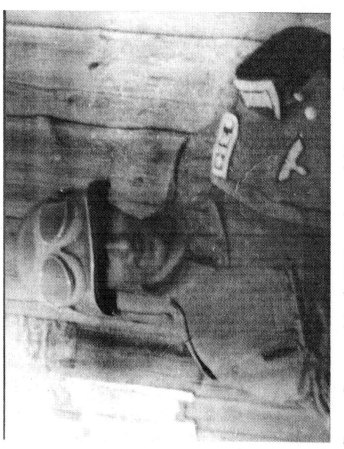

Siegen, Germany, March, 1945: author with his war collectibles. (Photographed by a "liberated" box camera).

Sudetenland, May, 1945: Sudeten Germans being evicted from their homes by the Czech National Police and sent to Germany. (Taken with a German box camera.)

American G.I.'s and Russian "Ivans" meet at Pilsen, Czechoslovakia May 8, 1945. (See Chapter 26.) (Taken with a German box camera.)

Paris, November, 1945: Criminal Investigator Livingstone on a deserter hunt. (See Chapter 27.)

Author's new "digs," Salzburg, Austria, 1952.
(See Chapter 38.)

Mirabel Garden, Salzburg, 1952: "Practical Lady" selling band concert tickets. Prize-winning print exhibited in the Smithsonian Institution and the Pentagon.

Self-portrait, Mirabel Palace, Salzburg, 1952.

"Harrow Boy" at Harrow School, near London, 1953.

"Coronation Broadcast." Listening to the "wireless" describing the Coronation of QueenElizabeth II, in Swanage, Dorset pub. Prize-winning print exhibited in the Smithsonian Institution and the Pentagon in 1954.

"Gemutlichkeit" - in an Austrian beer garden, St. Wolfgang, 1954.
Print published in British Annual of Photography collection, 1959.

Carmelites Lacy Williams and Steve Crouch at Point Lobos, California, 1958.

Walt Disney at La Playa Hotel, Carmel, California, 1960.

Boris Karloff, 1962. (See Chapter 47.)

Kim Novak and her mother, Carmel, 1963. (See Chapter 48.)

Salvation Army at Waldorf Astoria. New York, 1963.

From exhibition, "Jeff Walker's World," 1965.

Swiss soldier and son. Berne, Switzerland, 1970.

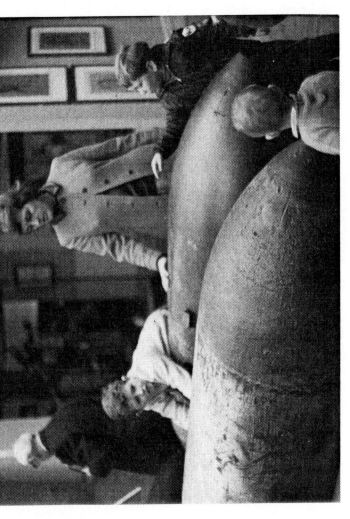

Imperial War Museum, London, exhibit of unexploded German bombs, 1970.

Avenches, Switzerland, 1970.

Carmel Mayor Clint Eastwood, 1982.

Guardia Civil, La Mancha, Spain, 1984. (See Chapter 43.)

Tom Sellick, 1998.

Place du Tertre, Montmartre, 2001.

28.

University Days

Late in the 1947 semester, Madison, Wisconsin was teeming with returning war veterans. Decent "digs" were in great demand, and in short supply. As we moved into our room, I tried to reassure my roommate, and myself, as well: "With twenty thousand veterans crammed into this town, we're damned lucky to find this room, even if it is a former funeral parlor."

Bob looked around the small "viewing" room and sniffed his disapproval. Heavy burgundy-colored drapes gave off a nagging odor of dead flowers with overtones, real or imagined, of formaldehyde vapors. I had once visited a medical student friend in a dissecting room at Science Hall. It was noontime, and he was standing at the bared feet of a cadaver, eating a sandwich. The dissecting room had a lot in common with our new room. The drapes covered most of the church-like stained glass leaded windows that opened out to the roar of traffic on University Avenue.

Our new landlady had turned her late husband's once thriving funeral business into a students' rooming house. It was a predictable, comfortable income for her and her daughter, though the high-spirited carryings-on of the younger students were getting on her nerves. She seemed relieved to have me and Bob as roomers. "You're older and more mature than the others. You'll keep them in line, won't you?" She pleaded.

We weren't thrilled with the room nor with the prospect of having to maintain order and quiet on a pride of young hell-raising lions bent on enjoying to the fullest their first year at the University. We decided to take the room on a week-to-week basis until we found something better. Two small cots and a couple of Salvation Army Modern desks and chairs were to be our "home" away from home. I hoped my mother would never see the place. I could just hear her say, "You didn't fight a war to come back to a flop-house. My son the veteran deserves better."

By semester's end, with no better accommodations in sight, Bob and I were beginning to feel resigned to our fate. But a Swedish exchange student I had met at the University's International Club told me he would be giving up his room at "Svenska Hus" and was returning home. I pounced upon the possibility of escaping the morbid fragrances and the din of our "viewing room" for something more comfortable, more civilized.

Berndt, my Swedish friend, confided to me, "Svenska Hus is on Langdon Street, near the campus, overlooking the lake. It's very nice inside, only the landlady, well she's – "

"We'll take it!" I interjected, my mind's eye presenting a picture of an old mansion along Fraternity Row, with large, airy rooms and maybe even a view of the lake.

"If you want it, " Berndt advised, "You'd better go there right away. It won't last long. It's expensive, though, eight dollars a weeks." The high price didn't put us off.

"Hang the expense! That's a lot more than we're paying here, but we're tired of all the traffic noise and thumping of adolescent shoes and drunken parties upstairs and down the hall. We'll take it sight unseen. I'll call the landlady and notify her. What's her name, Berndt?"

143

"Countess Britta Lundquist. You'll find her *interesting*!" Berndt dashed off on one of his calling cards her phone number and handed it to me, saying, "Lots of luck!"

Now, with the benefit of hindsight, Berndt's parting remark had an ominous ring to it.

I called Svenska Hus, and a man with a Brooklyn accent answered, not what I had expected.

"Yeah, we got a two-room deal widda connecting bath. The owner she tole me to pick up you guys at your house at seven tonight. She says you got a good reference from Berndt. You gotta move in tonight or you lose it, she tole me to tell ya."

Almost impulsively I shouted into the phone, "We'll take it! Can you pick us up at 2224 University Avenue?"

"Be all packed and ready to go. I can't make no more than one trip so you guys be ready there with everything packed. Okay?"

"Okay. We'll be out in front at seven sharp. Thanks."

"That was kind of reckless, Jack, taking that place sight unseen. I hope we won't regret it," Bob said.

"I guess this place is so depressing that any place would be an improvement. Besides, you know what a high-class guy Berndt is. He wouldn't live in just any place. No, my feeling is that it's going to be ten times better at only twice the cost. Besides, Bob, how often do you have the chance to get a Countess for a landlady?"

A gleaming tan Lincoln Continental convertible pulled up to the curb in front of our funereal rooming house. A short, swarthy, hairy man wearing a chauffeur's cap got out of the car and walked up to the entrance where Bob and I were waiting.

"Are you the guys moving into Britta's?" He asked.

"Yep," we replied in unison.

"Britta sent me over to pick up you and your stuff an' move you into the house."

"You call her Britta?" Bob asked.

"That's her name, ain't it?"

"You don't call her Countess? I asked.

"Nah! What for? This here's America! I'm Carlo, Axel's driver, handyman, gardener and watchdog. Pleased to meetcha, boys!"

Carlo had a permanent smile on his face. At first it made you wonder if anything he said could be taken seriously. He seemed good-natured, genial, even jovial.

While Carlo jammed our boxes of books and suitcases into the trunk, we climbed into the rear seat of the open car, after the overflow landed on the front seat. We took one last look at the dreary, noisy ex-funeral parlor that we had called home for four months. No more near-adolescents to sober up, no more roar of traffic outside our window, no more dead flowers' aroma seeping out of the drapes and curtains.

A feeling of well-being took hold, and Bob handed me a cigar he had saved for some such occasion. We both sat grandly in the back seat, gently tapping ashes over the side of the car, and waving nonchalantly to a couple of astonished classmates as we passed by.

Stopping for a traffic light, Carlo, his white-white teeth gleaming, shouted back to us, "You guys gonna have one helluva time at Britta's!"

"Is that a warning or a promise?" I asked, not at all sure how to take his meaning.

145

"You guys like excitement? You gonna have plenty!" Carlo went back to his driving, chuckling to himself.

"What's she like, the Countess?" I asked.

"She can be nice, she can be bad. Just don't never get her mad at you, that's all. When she gets mad, she stays mad."

"By the way." I asked, "Who's Axel?"

"You be seeing him on weekends. He's a *big* and I mean *big* building contractor. He poured the cement for a lotta the skyscrapers in Chicago. He come over here from Sweden with a bag of plumber's tools when he was fifteen, and now he's a real big shot. Britta calls him 'Uncle Axel'. He's no more her uncle than I am. He's over sixty now, but still big and strong. Don't cross him neither, guys."

I had never seen a real live Countess before. What would she look like? In my mind's eye she was tall, slender, blonde, wearing an expensive dress or riding clothes.

Carlo led the way up to a heavy iron-banded front door and let himself in with his own key. "Hey Britta!" He shouted, "Your two new roomers are here!" Bob and I looked at each other, wondering how a mere chauffeur could get away with such familiarity.

A short, thin woman in her early fifties came down the staircase to the entrance hall. She had dark hair streaked with grey, and wore a plaid shirt tucked into a too tight pair of blue jeans. If we had expected a cordial greeting, we were disappointed. The corners of her mouth were turned down even as she managed a wan semi-smile that deepened two long lines, the kind of lines that middle-aged men are bound to get from years of smoking a pipe. For what seemed to last a whole minute, she focused her gaze on each of us, from head to toe, and even on our luggage. Remembering that I hadn't taken time that morning to clean my fingernails, I quickly turned my fingers up into my palms. I hadn't expected so thorough a scrutiny.

There was something so very familiar about that woman. Could it be that we'd met before? The same lined face, the same hair, the same commanding presence! Now I remember! That arrogant German woman during the war. Frau Dalli. She's a dead ringer for Frau Dalli! That was two years ago during the Rhineland campaign, in Stolberg. We had breached Hitler's West Wall, swept through Aachen and occupied a factory town called Stolberg. We were setting up our battalion command post in the town's most impressive house. Our Colonel believed, with some justification, that the best house invariably belonged to the biggest Nazi in town. He preferred to inconvenience the town's *best* families by taking over their homes, giving them fifteen minutes to vacate the premises.

Earlier that morning we had taken a look at the Dalli family's factory. It was then manufacturing bars of shaving soap for the Wehrmacht. I can never forget what met our eyes there. About a dozen slave laborers were lying shivering on a cold concrete apron in the factory yard. Their only shelter from the elements was a corrugated metal roof. The "walls," for want of a better description, were nothing more than a coiled barbed wire fence. I walked over to a concrete guard box which had a small horizontal slit through which the guard could observe his "charges," even during an air raid. Behind the guard box was an entrance to a bomb shelter with a sign above it proclaiming, "Nur für Deutschen!" (Only for Germans!). I picked up a short wooden-handled whip with five or six leather thongs, each tipped with a lead ball. I was about to tuck it under my field jacket, a souvenir to

147

take home from Germany, but Colonel Brannan's eyes were quicker than my hand. From then on the whip hung by a thong from his jeep's windshield hinge, a constant reminder why we were over there making life difficult for our enemy.

The laborers were emaciated, hardly able to raise themselves from the concrete floor. Our medics were sent in to care for them and to get them decent shelter. One of the living skeletons waved a crumpled tiny Greek flag to welcome us into the enclosure. He even managed a smile. Our anger and hatred for our enemy somehow justified what punishment we were meting out with our artillery and bombers.

Once back at the Dalli mansion, I was detailed to move the Colonel's field desk and command post switchboard into the master bedroom on the second floor. The lady of the house, Frau Dalli, a greying, short, horse-faced woman, was methodically gathering up her clothes and ordering her maid to carry downstairs her suitcases. Striding up to the Colonel, she barked at him in good English, "Make sure your barbarians don't touch my antiques!"

Our C.O., hands on his hips and his jaw thrust out further than I'd ever seen it, his voice hoarse with anger, shouted, "Listen, and listen good, you G-dammed Kraut, I give the orders around here! Now get your German behind out of here before I order you shot!"

Frau Dalli, unaccustomed to such directness, blanched and slithered away down the hallway to the staircase. Then Colonel Brannan turned to me. I was pushing Frau Dalli's heavy, ornately inlaid wooden sewing machine down the hall toward the stairs, wondering how I would be able to get it downstairs and into a wagon waiting in the court yard. The Colonel, seeing me struggling with the machine, yelled at me, "Livin'stun, ole man, where the the hell you think you're goin' with that sewin' machine?"

"Sir," I answered, "She said she wanted it taken downstairs and put into the wagon outside."

"She's in a hurry, dammit! Send it to her airmail!" My Colonel snapped, pointing to an open window in the hallway.

After a moment's hesitation, grasping the meaning of his metaphor, I found the strength to lift the sewing machine up to the window ledge and to send it hurtling down two stories below. Frau Dalli's pride and joy smashed to bits on the cobblestones.

"There is some fun in wartime after all," I thought.

I never saw the likes of Frau Dalli again, that is, until I faced her near-duplicate at Svenska Hus in Madison two years later.

~~~

29.

First Encounter

Bob and I sat down in leopard skin-covered easy chairs facing our new landlady, who stood in front of the fireplace. She had in one hand a rhinestone-encrusted cigarette holder, and in the other, a tall frosted glass, nearly empty. She said in her sing-song accent, "Now boys, let's get off on a good start. Have a drink!" She was pouring a pitcher of scotch and ice into two more tall glasses and then her own. My eyes wandered over the room. It was large, oak-panelled, garishly though expensively furnished. The décor reflected our landlady's imperious, domineering temperament. It was sensual, intimidating. Thick oriental rugs clashed almost audibly with a leopard skin-covered sofa and easy chairs. A life-sized portrait – no mistaking it for anyone other than her mother – glowered down from above a massive pink marble fireplace. Two chubby cherubs in alabaster supported the mantle on which rested a large silver-mounted Viking drinking horn.

"What shall we call you? Countess? Mrs. Lundquist?" I asked, eager to put my best foot forward.

The Countess managed a fleeting smile and said, "The one thing I like about these Uniteh-States is that you Americans are not afraid to use first names. You are not so stiff and formal like ve are in Sveden. Vhen you are in the Hus, yust call me Britta, and Countess vhen ve're outside the Hus. I vill call you by your first names inside and outside the Hus."

We both nodded in agreement.

"Now, boys, Svenska Hus has some rules, wery simple rules. First, I rent only to yentlemen from good background. No rough Hus tolerated. You must ask my permission to have a guest come in, and no vomen except here in the liffingroom. Also, you pay your rent every Monday, eight dollars. You pay late and out you go. Understood?"

"Understood, Britta," I answered, uneasy about using her first name for the first time.

Svenska Hus was an old, yet well maintained mansion on Langdon Street, where fraternity houses and sorority houses vied with one another for outward dignity and elegance. Our two-room suite was on the second floor at the back of the house, looking out to Lake Mendota and the hills on the far side. Our sitting room had a fireplace over which Britta had posted a handwritten notice, "No fires." I hung over the fireplace a pleasant oil painting of a harbor scene my mother had given me to cheer up our previous digs.

~~~

30.

Breakfast with Britta

It was nine in the morning, and I was on my way to the Memorial Union for my bear claw and coffee. As I stopped in the front hall to put on my coat, I heard Britta's commanding voice:

"Yak! Come in here and choin me!"

(Dare I refuse? I thought.)

Britta was seated in front of the fireplace, with a roaring fire causing smoke to seep into the room. Her hair was carefully coiffed, unusual for this time of day, and she was wearing more rouge than usual.

"You expecting guests, Britta?" I had noticed fresh flowers, rolls and coffee set on the table.

She smiled. "Yust you, Yak." The way she called me "Yak" always made me cringe inside. Her steady gaze made me uneasy. "I have a class at ten, so I apologize for having to eat and run."

Britta ignored my attempt to escape. "Tell me something. Vhen you vere in Paris, you must have known a lot of vomen."

I suspected she meant "known" in the Biblical sense, but I wasn't about to ask. "In my job over there, tracking down black market operators and deserters, I didn't have many chances to meet a very wholesome kind of woman. They were mostly bar girls and street walkers. I did date an American Red Cross club director, and I liked her a lot, but she was transferred to Rheims, and I didn't see her much after that."

"Then you had opportunities to, shall ve say, 'sample the merchandise?"

"Oh, no, Britta. I was scared to death of V.D.! I wouldn't have touched any of them with a ten-foot pole! When we raided brothels, I always wore gloves, and I took a lot of razzing about it. My fellow C.I.D. agents got to calling me 'Virtuous John'."

"You vere wery vise for so young."

"We had a big chart on our wall in our office. It showed a high incidence of venereal disease cases reported in Paris each week. It was scary."

"I agree vith you. One cannot be too careful. I vould never let a man make love vith me vithout, you know, protection." Her usual pale complexion looked rosier than usual, and I didn't need a third eye to see what she was leading up to. I gulped down my coffee and looked at my watch, pretending to be surprised at how late it was. "Good grief! I'm due at the Armory in ten minutes! I'll just make it if I run. Thanks for your hospitality and your conversation."

Britta, smiling sweetly, replied, "Ve must have breakfast together another time soon, vhen you haff more time."

Britta offered her hand, something she had never done before. I gave her a hearty, firm handshake, something my father had taught me when I was very young. She let go of my hand decisively and quickly, not what I expected.

"Remember, Yak, it's your turn to escort me to the Klaab tonight."

I had completely forgotten about it; but I said with a parting smile, "Oh, yes, I'm looking forward to it." I hurried out the door.

Britta's "Uncle" Axel was a member, and his "niece" was allowed to dine at his club only if escorted. Everything went on his bill, but it wasn't something I was particularly fond of doing. It made me feel like a gigolo.

"It's going to be a long evening," I said under my breath, resisting the impulse to use the word "night."

~~~

31.

Dinner at the "Klaab"

Britta's once-a-week social occasion was to dine at the "Klaab," as she pronounced it. Each week it fell to one of us "boys" to escort her. At first the idea of a free dinner in elegant surroundings had a certain appeal. But there turned out to be a heavy price for the privilege: putting up with Britta's temper tantrums and her alcohol-fueled aggressiveness in meeting members of the "Klaab."

It was my night to escort my landlady to the "Klaab." Britta, in a particularly petulant mood, started off the evening with bawling out the cab driver for honking his horn in front of Svenska Hus instead of walking up to the front door and ringing the bell. The driver, having been previously exposed to Britta's tongue-lashings, was in no mood for further commentary from her. After she had noticed that he had run through a yellow traffic light and demanded to know why, the driver stopped the car and said,

"If you don't like the way I drive my cab, lady, get out and walk!"

We were still more than a mile from the "Klaab."

I smoothed things over by apologizing for her, and we managed to reach our destination without further trouble.

Upon entering the dining room, Britta spotted a portly, grey-haired man seated with an attractive, well-groomed lady about his same age. Britta summoned a waiter and asked, "I haff seen that couple here before. Who are they?"

"Governor and Mrs. Oscar Rennebohm, ma'am," was the reply.

Motioning the waiter to stay, Britta rummaged through her hand bag until she found one of Axel's business cards, and wrote on it, "With my compliments, Countess Lundquist." Handing the card to the waiter, she ordered, "Ask them to order from the vine list their favorite vine, and charge it to Mr. Lundquist's bill."

The waiter delivered the card to the Governor's table. The governor, having witnessed some of Britta's tantrums on previous occasions, read the card, showed it to his wife, and after a hurried, earnest discussion, nodded and smiled at their benefactor.

"They could haff at least come ofer to my table to thank me!" Britta huffed.

When the waiter returned to take our order, Britta said, "Vaiter, the last time I ordered the filet mignon, it was full of garlic, garlic all over it! This time, no garlic!"

I ordered the same entree; not wishing to antagonize my hostess, instructing the waiter to leave off the garlic on mine as well.

By the end of the meal, Britta had finished off several highballs, and began glaring at the Governor, hoping his eyes would meet hers. But he was engrossed in conversation with his wife, and having no apparent desire to fraternize with Britta, motioned to the waiter for his bill, signed it, and arose from the table to leave. The Rennebohms had to pass by Britta's table to leave the dining room, and Britta was not about to let them pass without a confrontation. Britta shot up from her chair as they approached, and motioned to me to do the same.

"Did you enchoy the vine I sent ofer to you, your Mayesty?"

The Governor, flustered, looked at his wife and then turned to Britta and replied, "Yes, Countess. That was a very kind gesture. Thank you very much."

Britta thrust out her hand, and he responded by taking her hand. Not wishing to release her grip, she pumped his hand, and said, "Your Mayesty, it is an honor to meet the governor off the best state in these Uniteh-States!"

Embarrassed and seemingly struggling to find the right response, the Governor replied, "You're too kind, Countess!" Extricating his hand from Britta's, he guided his wife toward the door. Mrs. Rennebohm hurried ahead of her husband, not wishing to prolong their encounter with Britta any longer than necessary.

All the way home in the taxi, Britta was grumbling about the Governor's aloofness and lack of appreciation for the "vine." It continued to be her favorite topic during her nightly "Svedish highball" – sparked monologues for several nights afterward. Then one night, enlarging on the subject, she said to Bob and me, "Guess who came ofer this afternoon, drunk, and vhen I vouldn't let him in, he vent around to my bedroom vindow and sang 'Some Enchanted Effening'?"

I ventured a guess: "Your Uncle Axel?"

"No! No! No! It vas Goffernor Rennebohm! Drunk like a skunk!"

I thought, (Axel's lawyer will be kept busy with Britta spreading this all over Madison!)

A Chat with the Governor

A week after Britta's revelation, Bob and I went to Janesville to a District Caucus of the Wisconsin Young Republicans, representing the University's chapter. Governor Rennebohm was the first speaker, who introduced the keynote speaker, Senator Joe McCarthy. In a monotone having the flavor of a dirge, McCarthy's speech should have been anything but rousing, but it was *what* he proclaimed, rather than *how* he proclaimed:

"The State Department, one of our nation's most important departments, is infested with communists. . .we're finding them infesting, like termites, the Army as well. . .nor do we have to look very far from here, to that great seat of learning, the University of Wisconsin, to find a nest of communist professors and students who must be recognized for what they are, sowers of treachery and deceit!"

The delegates applauded wildly; some even jumped to their feet. Caught up in the excitement, they stood shouting and applauding with their cupped hands to make the loudest possible applause. The senator's sweeping, tar-brush accusations and the near-hysterical response from his audience reminded me of newsreels I had seen of Hitler working up his followers in a crowded beer hall.

On the way out of the hall, I said to Bob, "That guy is a first-class rabble rouser! Even if he's proven right about ten percent of all those he's accusing of being communists, what about the damage he's doing to the other ninety percent who probably aren't? He can get away with making reckless accusations. Being a senator, he's immune from libel suits."

As we left the hall we noticed the Governor heading toward his limousine parked in front. I elbowed Bob, and pointing to the Governor, I said, "Let's have a chat with Oscar about Britta!" Bob gleefully agreed. We walked up to him as his wife was entering the car. "Governor, may we discuss a serious matter with you?" I asked.

"By all means. What's on your mind, fellows?"

"It's about Countess Lundquist. You met her recently at the Club. Well, she's spreading a malicious piece of gossip around town about you. We thought you should know."

"Just what is she saying, boys?"

I chimed in: "She's telling everybody who will listen that you came over to her house one afternoon, recently and – " I hesitated, trying to find the most accurate rendition of her story.

"And? Go on, tell me!"

"And that you were drunk, tried to get into the house, and when she wouldn't let you in, you went to under her bedroom window and sang "Some Enchanted Evening."'"

The Governor, visibly shaken by the disclosure, said, "Please get into the car and tell Mary, my wife what you've just told me!"

He introduced his wife to us and pointed to a pair of jump seats facing her in the back of the limousine. "Sit down, boys, and tell Mrs. Rennebohm what you just told me! Mary, I want you to hear from their own lips the damndest thing I've ever heard! Tell her, boys!"

I repeated the story, and Mrs. Rennebohm, calm under the circumstances, said, "Now we all know this to be a complete lie. Thank you for telling us about this. Every week since we met her at the Club, she has been sending us notes inviting us for cocktails at her house. She recently sent us a case of Scotch along with another invitation. We were on the verge of accepting her invitation! It was so dear of you to share this with us! Thank you!"

We left the limousine pleased with ourselves, confident we had done the right thing by the Governor of the best state in these United States.

"We sure fixed Britta's clock, didn't we?" I gloated all the way back to Svenska Hus.

~~~

32.

Britta's Christmas

A printed card on our door announced, "Guests should bathe daily since we have to kiss your ass to get along with you. (signed) The Management."

Bob had picked up the card at a roadhouse in northern Wisconsin. The inn evidently catered to a less than sophisticated clientele.

I hadn't noticed what Bob had posted on our door; I would have raised the issue of taste about it. Anyway, according to Carlo, guests of Britta's did take notice of the message. A Baron and Baroness from Sweden were occupying a room down the hall. One morning, Britta heard loud noises up on the second floor, and rushed upstairs to investigate. The Baron and his wife, almost doubled over laughing, pointed to the card. The Baroness, wiping tears from her cheeks, asked, "Britta, just when will you be kissing our behinds?"

The Baron added, "We promise to be freshly bathed if you give us advanced notice!"

Carlo, who had been dusting in the hall at the time, told us that Britta marched down the stairs cursing in Swedish.

When Bob and I returned home from the library that night, we faced a front door plastered with signs, big and small,: "Who is the Management!" and "*I* am the Management!"

The Importance of Being from Oshkosh

The door didn't open to our key. It had been bolted shut from inside the house. Bob managed a sheepish grin:

"Jack, I think something must've ticked off Britta."

We slept on the floor that night in Carlos' quarters above the garage.

Britta spent most evenings alone, reading "Vogue" or "Harper's Bazaar," and sipping her tall "Swedish highballs" while listening to Wagner. The high point of the day for her and the low point for us was when we "boys" came home from the library, staying there until the librarian practically evicted us at closing time. When we got home we'd quietly take off our shoes and tiptoe up the stairs in the hope that our landlady had dozed off in her chair. It didn't always work. If she was still awake, we were in for one of her "nightcaps," and one of her often repeated monologues: her great lost love, and of her "chewel" robbery, the greatest "chewel" robbery in these Uniteh-States."

About a week before Christmas, as we were tiptoeing up to our room, we were stopped dead in our tracks by a shrill, "Boys, come in here!" Britta was setting up a Christmas tree. "I've got a little yob for you. Halp me trim the tree!"

We spent about an hour placing the lights and ornaments, and were about to go upstairs when Britta said, "I'm giffing a Christmas party for you boys and your girl friends. On the eighteenth, the day before you go home." We accepted her command-like invitation, not without misgivings, more out of sympathy for this woman, whose only close friend was Axel, who hadn't been to see her in over a month.

"Will Axel be here for the party? Bob asked.

"Yes, he's promised to be vith me over Christmas so I von't be all alone in this great big Hus."

I felt relieved to hear it; Britta would be on her best behavior with her big "uncle" present. It won't be so bad, I thought, and besides, both Clara and Bonnie, having heard so much about our Swedish Countess, would be eager to witness this phenomenon themselves.

My own misgivings about the party made up all the basic ingredients of a self-fulfilling prophesy.

The night of the party, as Clara and I arrived, Britta was standing in her doorway, her breath giving off steam in the cold night air. She hadn't met Clara before, but I had told her that Clara was an exchange student from Norway. Our hostess was encased in a bright velvet gown, holding her cigarette holder in one hand and one of her tall Swedish highballs in the other. She managed a fleeting smile, and looking over Clara carefully, delivered a cool, nasal greeting: "Valcome to Svenska Hus, and Merry Christmas."

As we entered the living-room, I was glad to see Bob already there with Bonnie, standing by the fireplace, nursing one of Britta's highballs. "Sit down, everybody. I'll be back in a few minutes," Britta said quietly, as she disappeared into her bedroom across the hall from where we were standing.

"She's left to change into another evening gown," Bob said. This is the third change. You should have been here for the first two – a regular fashion show we're getting."

"Where's Axel? He was supposed to be here."

"Search me! No sign of him yet."

Clara and Bonnie looked around the room.

"See I told you, it's elegant and garish," I told Clara.

"Garish? I don't know that word. My English isn't all that good."

" 'Garish' means, well, you know the German word 'Kitsch'? In bad taste, that's what I mean, gaudy, showy."

Clara laughed. "Now I understand."

Britta made her entrance wearing a blue and silver sequinned gown this time. I thought that it might be appropriate to compliment her on her extensive and expensive wardrobe, after all the trouble she had gone to. "Britta, each gown makes you look even more beautiful than the last."

Britta looked at Clara, and said, "Clara, my dear, and where did you buy that dress? It's from Norway isn't it? I can always tell when something's from Norway."

"Oh, I bought this last week at Marshal Field's in Chicago. What a wonderful department store!"

I knew what was coming next. Anytime "Chicago" was mentioned, that was Britta's cue to tell about how she lost her "chewels" at the Palmer House in Chicago the first night she was in the "Uniteh-States."

"I hate Chicago! I'll nefer go back there as long as I live! Do you know vhy? I'll tell you. The first night I am in the Uniteh-States I am staying in the Palmer Hus. I go down to the dining room for dinner and to hear the string quartet. Then I go back to my room and what do I find when I go into my room? Everything torn apart out of my suitcases! All my best chewels gone! The greatest chewel robbery in these Uniteh-States! I'm so mad I want to go back to Sweden on the next plane, but Axel has already bought this house for me and told me there were less crooks in Madison. And you, Clara, what do you think of these Uniteh-States?"

Clara, flattered by her hostess's sudden show of interest, replied, "Oh, Countess, I'm so impressed with this big, powerful country! I'm glad to be here, aren't you?"

Britta retorted: "Big means nothing at all. Qvantity is not important, qvality is! Look at Sveden. Look at Chermany! Don't look at these Uniteh-States! What do you find here? I tell you what: terrible waitresses, loussy cab drivers, and everywhere criminals. I must tell you about one of my rings that vas stolen. It was giffen me by a German War hero, who came to Sveden after the Great War. We met in 1920 and we were lovers right away. Poor Hermann! He had so many var vounds that he almost liffed on morphine to kill the pain. He vanted to marry me, but my parents didn't like him because they thought he vas a nobody. 'How can somebody be somebody working in an airline office?' They would ask me. So I vaited too long to say 'Ja,' and vhat happens? That miserable little Baroness Katerina von Fock stole him from me. He married her and took her to Chermany. It lasted ten years, then she died on him! But no matter. Hermann had a good friend, Adolph Hitler, and in a few years he made Hermann the second most important man in the vorld, Ja. Hermann Goering! You may haff heard of him!"

Clara, her face becoming crimson, couldn't hold back. "I certainly have! He was a war criminal just as bad as Hitler, and he deserved to be hanged. By the way, Countess, if you don't like it here, why don't you go back to where you came from?"

Britta, jumping up from her seat, lashed out, "You little Norway snat, you are no longer velcome in my Hus! Get out!"

Clara and I bolted for the front door, picked up our coats, and not waiting to put them on, rushed out into the fresh night air. Then Bob and his date came out, shouting to Britta, "Thanks for an interesting evening. Merry Christmas!"

Since Britta's ill-fated Christmas party, her coolness toward me and Bob turned to icy cold. I couldn't wait to leave for home for the holidays. It would be my mother's first Christmas since Dad died, and I knew it was important to spend as much time with her as possible.

Mother and I were trimming our Christmas tree when the phone rang. As luck would have it, Mother got to the phone first. She heard a distraught, sobbing woman's voice: "Let me speak to Yak!"

"Who is speaking, may I ask?"

"This is Countess Lundquist, your son's landlady. I must speak vith him!"

Mother, her curiosity aroused, handed me the phone and raced to the kitchen where she picked up an extension phone.

Britta was sobbing. "Yak, oh Yak, I'm all alone in this great big Hus! Do you know how it is to be alone in this great big Hus? Axel was supposed to be with me for Christmas, but he yust flew to Sveden to see his dying brother. Please, Yak, stay with me at Christmas!"

Knowing my mother was in on the conversation made me nervous. My immediate reaction was to blurt out something like, "that's impossible! Good-bye!" And hang up, leave the house, and call her back from a public phone, but this would have increased my mother's suspicions.

"Britta," I said in the calmest voice I could muster, "I'm spending Christmas with my mother. There is no way I'm going to leave her alone at Christmas. Besides, the way you treated Clara at your party, I can't think of you as any kind of friend."

"Clara? Who is Clara? I don't remember any Clara, what are you talking about?"

"You know, Britta, you bring a lot of this being alone on yourself. I'm sorry you'll be alone at Christmas, but there is nothing I can do. Good-bye and Merry Christmas."

Britta started shrieking at me, and I slammed down the receiver. Mother came out of the kitchen and stared at me as if she didn't know me.

"Let's finish the tree, Mom," I said.

That little brush with Britta cast a pall over the rest of my vacation, but that was nothing compared to what awaited me on my return to Madison.

~~~

33.
McCarthy's Shadow

A recently commissioned second lieutenant in the Army Reserve, I attended drills and classes every Thursday night at the Reserve Center, off the university campus. During my first drill after returning from Christmas vacation, I was called off the floor and told to report to my C.O. He handed me a slip of paper which ordered me to report to a Colonel Bondin at his office in the State Capitol building, Monday, at 1500 hours.

A commendation? Certainly not a promotion this soon. Maybe a new assignment, or an invitation to join the Regular Army. Time will tell, I told myself.

At the appointed hour, in my pinks and greens, proudly wearing my two rows of campaign ribbons and with my lapel insignia freshly polished, I knocked on the frosted glass door of the Colonel's office. I was ushered into the presence of a red-faced, obese old Colonel of Infantry whose four rows of decorations made mine look meager. I saluted smartly. "Lieutenant Livingstone reporting as ordered, sir!"

The old man, slouched behind his bare desk, wanly, almost reluctantly returned my salute. I sensed that some kind of reprimand was in the offing. His thinning white hair and bent-over posture confirmed what I had heard, that he had survived the Bataan Death March and years in a Japanese prison camp. Shaking his finger at me, he bellowed, "You are to resign your commission, effective immediately!"

I couldn't have been more stunned than if I had been struck by lightning.

"Sir," I blurted out, "What's this all about? I just received my commission a few months ago. I haven't violated any army regulations. I have a right to know why you are ordering this!"

The Colonel, unaccustomed to being spoken to in that manner, didn't conceal his annoyance. His face growing even redder, he yelled at me: "As you well know, there's no place in the Armed Forces of the United States for communists or their sympathizers."

I groped for a proper response. "I'm no communist. I'm no communist sympathizer! Whoever accuses me of this is going to be sued for slander! If you took the trouble to investigate, you'd have found that I am an active member of the University of Wisconsin Young Republican Club. Believe me, sir, you'll be hearing from my parents' attorney! I'm preparing for a foreign service career, and an accusation like this could ruin my career even before it started. I'll bet I know where you got your information. She'll be hearing from my attorney as well!"

I spun around on my heel, not wanting him to see the tears of rage brimming in my eyes. I rushed out the door, and with the help of a strong draft from the corridor, the door slammed shut with a loud crash.

The next day I drove up to Oshkosh to see our family attorney, Richard Laus.

"What brings you here, Jack?"

"First of all, my mother must not know about this mess I'm in."

"Mess? What kind of mess?"

"Well, my landlady is slandering me all over Madison. She's telling people that I'm a communist, and an old addled-pated colonel has taken what she told him seriously, and has ordered me to resign my commission.

I've been working hard to get into the Foreign Service, and this cloud over me could ruin everything."

"First, about your mother finding out: as long as I don't have to bill your mother for my fees, there's no need to get her into the picture."

"Whew! I was more worried about that than almost anything else! I'll pay any legal fees out of the Trust income Dad left me."

"Now Jack, calm down and tell me why you think your landlady, Mrs.?"

"Lundquist, Britta. She's a Swedish countess. She's neurotic, an alcoholic, a vindictive troublemaker. Everywhere she goes, to everyone she meets, she brings trouble. Her so-called "uncle" Axel has an attorney in Madison on a retainer to try to keep her out of trouble. When she's been crossed, she just gets plain nasty. She smokes like a chimney, drinks like a fish, she's full of venom and – "

"I get the picture, Jack. Now let's get specific. Just what did you do to cross her?"

"My date and I walked out on her Christmas Party when she insulted her, and while I was home with Mom during Christmas vacation, she called me, pleading and crying over the phone, to go back to Madison to spend Christmas with her. My mother heard the whole conversation on another line, and she suspects there's some sort of 'thing' going on between us. Well, I turned down Britta flat and hung up on her.

Some time ago, before Christmas vacation, my roommate and I had gone to a Janesville Young Republican caucus to hear a speech by Senator McCarthy. I thought McCarthy was a rabble-rouser, I told my roommate, who agreed, we talked about it all the way back to Madison. We were still discussing it when we got to the house, and Britta, our landlady heard me say that I thought McCarthy was an idiot, making false accusations about a lot of innocent people. She picked up on this, and is using it to smear me. I want to sue her and that old bastard, Colonel Bondin for slander!"

"Whoa up there, Jack. Tell me about this Colonel. Where does he come into this thing?"

"He knows her socially. They both go to the Madison Club. He's obviously not all there upstairs. He's a survivor of the Bataan Death March, and it's pickled his brain, if you ask me. He's retiring soon. The Army is putting him out to pasture, and this is probably his last assignment."

The attorney thought for a moment, then said, "Jack, *the higher up they are, the harder they fall.* He's probably looking forward to a pretty good retirement income, probably even another medal for all he's been through. He has more to lose than you do. Forget about suing him or your landlady. The more you stir up that sort of thing, with your landlady, I mean, the more it gets to smell. You don't need a lawsuit. Even if you won, you can't place any monetary value on a career you haven't even begun, so you'd be lucky to collect your legal costs and 'nominal' damages of two cents. What I'm going to do is to write a stern warning letter to your Colonel, demanding an immediate retraction of his order and an apology to you. Also, find out her attorney's name in Madison and I'll write him as well, promising no further action if he can get you moved out of the house and into other suitable accommodations right away. You should be hearing from both of them within a week. In the meantime, *Illigitimi non carborundum.*' Know what that means?"

"I haven't the slightest idea."

"Don't let the bastards wear you down."

A week later, I picked up a letter for me on the front hall table. The return address on the envelope made me catch my breath. It was from the Adjutant General's office, Army Reserve, State Capitol Building.

I gasped, "It's from that old S.O.B.!" I ripped open the envelope and read the contents:

"Subject: Request for Interview

To: Second Lieutenant John Livingstone, USAR

1. You are hereby requested to meet with the undersigned at 1300 hrs. 5 June, 1950 at this office.

(signed) Bondin, Col. Inf. USA

On the appointed day at the appointed hour, I reported to the Colonel's office, having "cleared the cobwebs" with a strong cup of coffee just before entering the Capitol Building. (He hasn't a leg to stand on, and the letter from Richard has him scared spitless! Like a cornered animal, he'll try to pull rank and buffalo me, but it won't work. *The higher they are, the harder they fall.* He has so much more to lose than I do, and he knows it!)

Buoyed up by these affirmations, I entered the Colonel's office and saluted my adversary.

"Second Lieutenant Livingstone reporting as ordered, Sir."

The Colonel got up from behind his desk and returned my salute with a lot more verve than the first time. Pointing to a chair with a shaky finger, he said, "Sit down, Lieutenant. Thank you for being punctual. I have another appointment in a few minutes so I'll make this as brief as I can. Evidently there has been a mistake, obviously a case of mistaken identity, a case of mistaken identity. A case of mistaken identity. It was another young officer, not you at all. Not you at all. Aren't you relieved? You know how Senator McCarthy has been finding communists under every rock, so to speak, under every rock, well we in the Army are not immune to his investigations. We can't be too careful, can we? That is to say, where there's smoke, there's fire, usually, that is. Where there's smoke there's fire. I apologize for being over-zealous in trying to protect the army. These days, one can't be too careful when national security is at stake. One can't be too careful, can one? Now Lieutenant, I've made my apology, and have explained how it happened. Your name has been cleared of any taint. You have a fine record, and it's going to stay that way. So, as far as I'm concerned, the matter is closed. The matter is closed."

The old man offered his hand, but I chose to ignore the gesture and replied, "Sir, thank you for clearing this thing up and for your apology. Would you please give me a written apology?"

The Colonel, his face turning ashen, replied, "Now Lieutenant, an officer's word is his bond. You don't need anything in writing. I must tell you, this affair has caused me a lot of problems. Mainly health problems. I'm not well, as you can see. Let bygones be bygones, eh, what do you say?"

(No sense in beating a dying old horse. – it's time to forgive, time to be charitable.) "I accept your apology, Colonel. You understand how important my future career plans are to me, and why I found it necessary to get legal help –"

"I understand, Lieutenant. Good luck to you."

"And good luck to you, sir." I saluted and left the office, feeling ten feet tall. This time the door closed quietly. "The higher they are, the harder they fall," I said over and over.

~~~

34.
Mother Meets the Countess

A week after my return from Christmas at home my mother phoned and said she'd meet me at the house in Madison and take me to lunch. When I got to the house, Mother had already arrived, and was standing under the chandelier in the entrance hall, her mink coat glistening under the lights. Britta made her entrance through the sliding door from the living-room. For what seemed close to twenty seconds, the two stood there, not missing any detail of each other's hairdo, jewelry, dress, and shoes. (Like two cats, ready for battle), I thought. Britta spoke first. "Velcome to Svenska Hus. As you can see, your son's accommodations are first class and *Svedish clean*. I am wery particular who rent rooms from me, and all my boys are perfect yentlmen."

My mother, always quick on the uptake, answered, giving me a sidelong glance, "Perfect gentlemen? I certainly hope so."

Britta took a deep puff on her cigarette, hesitated for a moment, trying to decide on how to cope with a formidable new adversary. She knew full well why my mother had come to Madison. Still standing in the hall, Britta got right to the point: "My uncle was supposed to come up from Chicago to spend Christmas with me, but he called me and said he had to see his dying brother in Sveden. I was wery upset to be alone in this great big Hus. The boys were away, so I started calling them to see if they could keep me company for a day or two. Your son was the last one I called, you know. You being a widow, I thought you would haff lots of family with

175

you. And I wass so alone in this great big Hus! Do you know what it's like to be alone in such a great big Hus? Well anyway, it's over."

I felt relieved that I wasn't the only one, or the first one to be called. Come to think of it, Bob hadn't mentioned a call from her, but then, out of embarrassment, I hadn't told him either.

Mother was about to reply, but I cut in. "Mom, let me show you my room and the view of the lake."

I led her up the staircase to the second floor. Once in the room, she nodded approvingly as she spotted a small framed portrait of her on the mantel just below the harbor scene painting she had given me. Her portrait was flanked by a tiny scale model of a 105 mm. Howitzer and a Pershing tank. Hanging on the wall alongside the harbor scene was an SS officer's dagger I had found while poking around in the ruins of an SS barracks at Berchtesgaden five years before. What touched her most was a small metal perfume bottle with a large dent in it. I had bought the bottle of perfume in Normandy while enroute to the front in Belgium, hoping to bring it home to her after the war. I carried it in my field jacket pocket. One cold December night in the Ardennes during a barrage of overhead bursts from German 88 mm.'s, I dove for cover, all of my weight landing on the corked bottle. The cork gave way, spewing the perfume into my pocket, and the bottle sustained a deep dent. For days my B.O. I had become accustomed to was masked by a fragrance that reminded me of hollyhocks and tear gas. My buddy on the observation post with me complained incessantly about "that smell," which, according to him, ". . . if the wind shifts in the Krauts' direction, it'll be all over for us in a few minutes."

I tried to calm him, suggesting, "If they get a whiff of this, they'll be coming to us without their weapons ready, expecting to find a bevy of Belgian whores, and we can pick them off, one by one."

After surveying the room and its decor, Mother said, "I feel better now that I've met the Countess. She seems harmless enough. But mind your P's and Q's, and for God's sake, don't have anything but a coke with her! If that landlady of yours gives you any trouble, I want you to find another place to stay right away."

I thought, (With 20,000 veterans combing the bushes for rooms, I can put up with Britta a little longer.)

"Okay, Mom, don't worry about her. I'm perfectly safe. Besides, I have Bob to protect me."

In the car on the way to the restaurant, Mother was unusually quiet. She had something important on her mind. I sensed it strongly. After lunch, when we got to the parking lot behind the restaurant, she began to unburden herself. "Jack, dear, how are you doing? What I mean is, how are your grades this semester? I worry all the time about that woman robbing you of your study time. Ever since that phone call at Christmas, I've had a nagging feeling about her. She could be trouble with a capital T. I want you to move out of there. I felt bad vibrations as soon as I entered that house."

"Mom, my grades are just fine. I'm carrying a bigger course load than last semester, and may not get another four-point this time, but it won't be far off that, I'm sure."

"I so want to be able to say one day, 'my son, the diplomat'. I couldn't be more proud of you. Mrs. LeDoit told me just the other day that you have what it takes to reach whatever goal you set."

(That's a safe prediction if I ever heard one), I thought. "As for moving out of Britta's house, finding another room this time of the year would take a lot of time, time I can't afford. Don't worry about her. She's carrying a lot of baggage. I'm sure she's homesick for Sweden, and not able to see her son, who's living with his father. Sure, she's neurotic, drinks too much, but Bob and I can cope with her. Anyway, since Christmas she's been very cool toward me, and I like it that way."

"Hell hath no fury like a woman burned," Mother said.

"You mean spurned."

"I'm alone most of the time since Dad passed on and when you went away to school. When you come home on an occasional weekend, I hardly see you, what with you being with your friends or your nose buried in books. I thought we ought to have this little chat about your future and my future. First of all, any little mistake can endanger your career plans. Before they hire for a government job, they'll check into your background with a fine-toothed comb."

"I have nothing to hide or be ashamed of, Mom. Let's talk about you, Mom."

"Jack, I know I can't hang on to you much longer. You'll be at Georgetown in the fall, completely on your own, so I've decided to sell the house and move out to California, away from these terrible winters and too hot summers. I never did like Oshkosh. I came from a different world, Texas, but I made the best of it, for your dad's sake. I'll never forget how we lost everything during the crash, and had to start over again. I've never told you about this before, but your dad had this 'thing' about making money from the war. As soon as the war started, your dad's business of salvaging high-speed steel borings made us wealthy almost overnight. When you joined the Army, Dad got obsessed with the idea that we were going to lose you over there, that any day there would come a knock on the door with a telegram. That was to be the price we had to pay for profiting from the war. I pleaded with him to go to church on Wednesday nights to hear all the wonderful testimonials about how many boys were being protected through prayer and knowing the Truth. You were protected beautifully, weren't you? Every day you were away, I called our C.S. practitioner, Mrs. Thresher. Remember her? When you were ten, she stopped that middle ear infection dead in its tracks, and you never had another. Had we let mortal mind take over, you could have been wounded, taken prisoner, or killed, but here you are, whole and sane, after all you went through over there, thank God! All that needless worry took its toll, Dad's heart attack."

"I feel responsible in a way."

"You're in no way responsible! You would have been drafted if you hadn't enlisted, and who knows what could have happened then? No, son, it was Dad's own erroneous thinking that shortened his life. Why he never joined the church I'll never know."

"Well Mom, your son the student has to bone up tonight for two exams tomorrow: Diplomatic History and Spanish Literature." I hugged her and kissed her cheek.

"Do well, and don't let that Swedish witch take you away from what's important. I trust you, dear!" She gave me a weak smile and drove off.

~~~

35.

A Brush with Officer Hammersley

It was a warm June evening on the campus of the University of Wisconsin. In a couple of weeks my four-years at Madison would culminate with my graduation with a B.A. in International Relations. Next stop: (so I thought) Georgetown University, where I hoped to be accepted for graduate studies in preparation for a Foreign Service career.

On my way to Elizabeth Waters Dorm to pick up my date, the lake-side path was alive with romantic couples walking languidly hand in hand toward Picnic Point, just beyond the boundaries of the university's beautiful, forested campus.

As we walked back after a leisurely dinner at the Memorial Union's Heidelberg-evoking Ratskellar, we were mindful of Pat's dorm's ten o'clock rule, when the dorm's doors would be locked for the night. We each in our own way dreaded parting so early. Breathing heavily, I venture to ask her, "We have twenty minutes before your curfew time. Let's get off this path and rest awhile. Okay?"

Pat needed no telepathic powers to sense what I wanted. "No, Jack, there's no time," she sighed, with little conviction in her voice. Taking her cue, I guided her off the path to a grassy miniature meadow screened from the path by trees and tall grass. This was to be our first, and last, as it happened, night of passion. As if by some primal instinct, we both seemed to know what to do, even back then in 1950, before the onslaught of explicit TV and movies. Just as our bodies were about to unite as one, I felt a cold, wet, soft object nudging my exposed posterior's right cheek. It was so startling it completely dampened my ardor. I looked up to see a grinning cocker spaniel, her tail wagging, held back by a leash in the hands of our popular campus cop, Officer Hammersley.

With an apologetic tone, our *coitus interuptor* feigning severity, declared, "I'm only doing my duty, as your parents want me to do. Take my advice, kids, don't try this sort of thing on the campus. If I catch you again, I'll have to turn your names into the Chancellor's office, and you know what that'll mean." He then proceeded with his spaniel down the path in search of further assignations.

~~~

36.

An Invitation

A week after my brush with Officer Hammersley's spaniel, a terse typewritten note arrived for me at Svenska Hus. The return address on the envelope was ominous: Office of the Chancellor. As I opened the envelope, my heart began pounding like a pile-driver. (That damned Hammersley didn't keep his word!) I was furious and scared at the same time, scared for my future chances of being accepted in the fall at Georgetown. I saw all my grandiose hopes and plans for a foreign service career going up into a mushroom cloud of dust and ashes. The note confirmed my fears: It requested me to report to the Vice Chancellor at one o'clock the following day. There followed a sleepless night during which I rehearsed over and over my pleas for understanding and for mercy.

After a stress-spoiled lunch at the Memorial Union's staid, stuffy Georgian Grill, wearing my best suit and bow-tie, my "ruptured duck" veteran's pin gleaming in my lapel button hole, I arrived at precisely one o'clock at the Chancellor's Office.

The Vice Chancellor greeted me with unexpected warmth, considering the occasion of my visit. I noticed that he had on his desk a copy of my university transcript. "Do you know why I've sent for you?" He asked.

"Yes, sir, I do." I replied, the muscles of my throat allowing only a whisper to pass.

With a quizzical look the Vice Chancellor studied me closely. "There must be a leak somewhere. This was to be strictly confidential."

(That 'somewhere' is Hammersley) I thought.

After a long pause, my host pointed to a chair, and asked me to sit down. He began, "Well, at any rate, this interview is to remain strictly confidential, you understand, not to leave this room for anybody's ears, right?"

"Oh, right! Absolutely!" I responded with enthusiasm. I couldn't help admiring the tact with which my case was being handled. Now I waited for the other shoe to fall.

"Mr. Livingstone, your army record and your transcript indicate you have prior training in military intelligence, that you are fluent in Spanish, and that you are getting your B.A. in International Relations. . . ."

(He certainly has a roundabout way of getting around to Hammerley's spaniel's cold nose. What do International Relations have to do with personal relations? I asked myself.)

The Vice Chancellor then put his cards on the table: "As the newly appointed campus recruiter for the Central Intelligence Agency, I'm authorized to invite you to apply for a worthwhile career in the CIA. You're invited to contact a Lt. Colonel Donald V. Mulcahy at this address in Washington. If you're interested, take this envelope along with you. Your trip to Washington, of course, will be at your own expense. Upon arrival there you will be scheduled for tests and a series of interviews to determine your suitability."

Barely able to conceal my feeling of relief, I thanked him and said yes, I would be interested if the pay were sufficient.

"Oh, the CIA pays well. Even while in training you'll be paid around three hundred dollars a month."

This was an offer hard to resist.

A week after graduation, only my mother, sworn to secrecy, knew of my trip to Washington. I arrived by train at Union Station, and reported to Lt. Col. Mulcahy that same day. His office was located in an old W.W. II "temporary" building along the reflecting pool in the center of Washington. At the reception desk I was handed an identification badge, and ushered into the colonel's office.

He greeted me cordially, with army recruiter-like enthusiasm, and explained to me the mission of the CIA, and what a great opportunity it would be to serve my country in this new, fast-growing service. Then he invited me to join him for lunch at the building's cafeteria. It was one of those cold, warmed-over leftover meals one would like to forget if only one could. I began to have my doubts about joining an organization that fed its people so badly. We sat in partitioned-off cubicles that contained only one table and two chairs in each. The sound-proof partitions guaranteed that no conversation could be heard past the partition.

"Since your training and past experience in military intelligence and your ability to speak Spanish are of potential value to us, if you are accepted for training, you'll be most likely sent to somewhere in Latin America."

I recoiled at this suggestion, and for good reason. "That's not possible, Colonel," I interrupted. "You may think this sounds strange, but back in 1943 I had a very realistic dream. I was in some pop-gun republic, in some tropical country, and was shot by a firing squad. The dream was so realistic, I've never forgotten it. It could have been prophetic.

I went to a clairvoyant, who told me that the dream was a warning, and that I should take it seriously."

Col. Mulcahy, bemused and surprised, replied, "Well, this severely limits your value to the Company as far as operations are concerned. Anyway, go ahead and take the tests tomorrow, and return home. We'll let you know one way or another within two weeks of our decision."

With that less than promising beginning behind me, the next morning I took a taxi to an unpretentious looking flat in Georgetown. In a crowded hallway I stood waiting to be called for testing along with a nondescript assortment of fellow invitees, each encased in a sheath of complete anonymity, not one daring to speak to another. It was as if prior to my arrival they all had been cautioned to have nothing to do with me or with each other. An odd-looking group of individuals, each a quintessential prototype of what I thought a spy should be like.

At the outset of the test, we were required to sign an oath to the effect that we were never to divulge any of the contents, nor even the very nature of the test to anyone. As I glanced at my fellow would-be spies, I wondered if this was the best choice I could have made. Georgetown might be, after all, a better, safer choice. Well, I thought, I'd gotten this far, so I may as well go on with this.

I left Washington for home the next day.

~~~

37.

And So Go the Slowa 1951-1952

The word *slowa* in Polish means *words*. During a year (1951-52) of near-total immersion in Polish at Presidio of Monterey's Army Language School our instructors poured into our overcrowded heads every day an increasingly long list of new *slowa*. My brain, for one, was like a tiny clothes closet, already tight with clothes, offering little space for more. Retrieving anything from that jammed closet became harder with each day.

Every morning at 0800 hours we were required to recite from rote memorization a full page of dialogue in Polish, incorporating all the new *slowa* from the previous day's list.

Any fantasy we may have entertained of socializing with ladies of the Monterey Peninsula soon evaporated. Our one, daily brief "happy hour" came after classes, from 4:30 to 5:30 down the hill at the Hotel San Carlos cocktail lounge. It was the only time we had to squander, away from those interminable vocabulary lists and dialogues. The war raging in Korea kept us all motivated not to fail the course.

Our daily "happy hour" was a source of mystery for my classmates. Almost daily an attractive blonde woman in her thirties would arrive, walk up to my table, whisper something in my ear, and hand me a key. Then she would leave as suddenly as she had arrived. Brushing off the inevitable questions with a brusk "no comment," I would then leave the lounge, drive up Carmel Hill to Frances' house and let myself in with her key. By the time I arrived she would have left on a date, and had placed two one-dollar bills on her mantle, my fee for "baby-sitting" her two children. My almost nightly "baby-sitting" netted me almost forty dollars a month, a welcome augmentation to a meager first lieutenant's salary. It also gave me peace and quiet, away from the noisy Bachelor Officers Quarters, to memorize those infernal vocabulary lists and dialogues.

Every month, like clockwork, just a week prior to payday I'd invariably run out of money, and would run down to the Bank of America on Alvarado Street and borrow fifty dollars to tide me over. On payday B of A promptly received back their fifty dollars plus ten dollars interest.

Getting back to memorizing Polish *slowa* by the dozens: there was the overwhelming problem of having to spell Slavic sounds with our Roman alphabet. The learned priests who brought the Roman alphabet and Latin to Poland didn't do the Poles any big favor. The Poles would have been far better off if they had imported the Cyrillic alphabet from their Russian neighbors. The Cyrillic alphabet is highly phonetic. Each Cyrillic letter is capable of making all those Slavic sounds intelligible to the eye far more efficiently than the Roman alphabet. Imagine having to memorize and pronounce a simple Polish word *przyjemność*, which means *pleasure* in English! Or, having a *sczeka* for a jaw and a *kegostup* for a spine. All this travail was giving me *bólglowy* (headaches).

I had recently heard about an effective method to aid rote memorization, a "sleep-teaching machine." It consisted of a tape recorder (big and heavy back then in

187

1951), a time-clock and a small loudspeaker to be placed under your pillow. I saved up three months' baby-sitting money to buy the contraption, pinning all my hopes on the miracle of sleep-teaching. In my BOQ room at the Presidio I set up the machine, and set the time-clock to start playing a half-hour-long new vocabulary list, repeated over and over, intended to bore itself into my subconscious mind while I was soundly asleep, every morning at three a.m. My BOQ had been built during the Spanish-American war, and the partitions between the rooms were thick, or so I thought. I was confident that my neighbor, Captain Hernandez, on the other side of the wall would not hear the barely whispered tape recording coming from under my pillow. What I hadn't counted on, however, was his big Irish Setter dog, Coco, whose keen hearing caught the low-decibel tape recording of Polish verbiage coming from under my pillow. At precisely three o'clock every morning she would commence howling and growling, waking up her master, prompting a stream of Spanish epithets from him which lasted until the tape ran out at three-thirty. I did the honorable thing, and turned off the three a.m. time-clock. The machine, during its short life, if it hadn't been for Coco, probably would have made recalling all those new words every morning easier; I'll never know for sure.

During my year at ALS I noticed what at first I attributed to be a cultural trait of Polish people. All my instructors, native-born Poles, seemed to have a pained expression much of the time. I attributed it to the fact that they had suffered under Nazi occupation, had suffered and escaped from communist oppression. It dawned on me toward the end of my year that there was yet another cause for their pain: the day-to-day slaughter of their beautiful Polish language by American tongues.

One of my instructors, Pan Kodrebski, had a particularly frequent pained expression, no matter how hard I tried to pronounce my Polish words correctly. Another instructor, Pan Majdanski confided in me,

"Pan Kodrebski was a Major in the Polish cavalry, and was one of the few who were not mowed down when they charged German tanks with their lances. He was taken prisoner, tried to escape, and a German guard struck him in his back with his rifle butt. He still winces in pain because of that injury. Don't worry about your pronunciation, It's just fine!"

Macej Radziwil, a former prince of illustrious Lithuanian noble origin, was one of my instructors. His wife, Christina accepted their lot in life as refugees in a strange new country with courage and stoicism, and through the years of their life on the Monterey Peninsula was a constant and devoted volunteer at the local hospital.

Tadeusz Haska escaped from a political prison in Poland, reached Sweden, and went back to spirit out his wife, rowing a small boat in the Baltic to reach freedom in Sweden.

As for slowa by slowa, after a year of packing my cranium with seemingly thousands of unspeakable Polish nouns, adjectives, adverbs and verbs, I was sent to Salzburg, where nary a Polish word was heard.

~~~

38.

A Well-kept Secret 1952

The day after arriving in Salzburg, Austria, I reported in at my newly assigned intelligence unit's headquarters at Lehener Kaserne, a former German Army barracks along the Salzach River. I was assigned to preside over and protect the contents of an office filled with filing cabinets. At the top of each cabinet was taped a thermite grenade. The grenades were placed there in the event of a sudden invasion by our neighbors close by, the Soviet Army. I soon learned that as my unit's new Documents Security Officer I was responsible for the safeguarding of thousands of linear feet of classified documents, churned out by our unit's far-flung collectors, evaluators, interpreters, analysts, paper-pushers of every conceivable level of erudition and non-erudition. Just by pulling the pins of the thermite grenades, they would burn so fiercely that they would go straight down through the steel cabinets and destroy their contents within a few minutes, probably taking the whole building along with the files as well. Another of my duties consisted of escorting selected documents down to our incinerator on the bank of the Salzach river, watching and accounting for every sheet consigned to the flames, witnessing the stirring of the ashes and dumping of the ashes into the river, a routine that occurred once every week.

In the 1950's we had no copy machines worthy of the name: only mimeograph machines which could be used only for unclassified information, and carbon paper for reports. You could always spot our "paper-pushers" by the tell-tale carbon paper smudges on their thumbs and forefingers. I quickly became a part of that vast fraternity.

My immediate superior, Major Norwood, was a taciturn, soft-spoken professional, seemingly unflappable. The Major summed up my new situation:

"This being an intelligence unit in close proximity to the Soviet Army and its intelligence apparatus, you'll appreciate that we must at all times operate under a strict system of S.O.P's (standard operating procedures). Telephone communication to our units in the Salzkammergut (Lake District), Linz, and Vienna is limited to non-classified information. Everything else is put on paper and delivered by couriers. This first week you'll be able to get away from the office and visit our detachments all over the U.S. Zone and in the International Sector of Vienna. Any travel through the Soviet Zone carries certain risks, which we do our best to keep to a minimum. It'll take time to acclimate yourself to this business, but you'll pick it up fast."

Soon after arriving in Salzburg, I was temporarily billeted at a small, undistinguished hotel, the Pitter, near the railway station. The gloomy room looked out over a run-down part of the city, where bomb damage still had not been completely cleared away. I spent as little time as possible in my room, and during my free hours roamed all over the old part of the city, snapping pictures of the wonderful architecture and of the people in the streets, rebuilding their city and their lives in the aftermath of the war. The army had set up a darkroom for us photographers a few steps away from our main and best officer's hotel, the *Oesterreischischerhof.*

The Importance of Being from Oshkosh

The "O.H." as we quickly learned to refer to it, had a charming open-air terrace restaurant facing the Salzach River and the huge, grey *Festung*, (fortress) on top of a cliff on the other side of the river. A pianist played softly in the background, and influenced by the refined, cultured ambience, the officers and their guests spoke in hushed tones.

It was my favorite place for an evening meal and a glass of wine before returning to my drab room at the Pitter.

I was seated alone one evening in the O.H., when an elderly couple, elderly for me at the time, a couple in their sixties, walked up to my table and said hello. I had met them on the ship coming over, and we had some pleasant conversations about Austria, about which I knew practically nothing, and they knew practically everything, having been stationed there for several years. They found me a good listener, eager to soak up as much information as I could.

"What are you up to, John?" Karl, the husband asked.

Not about to talk shop with near-strangers, I decided to make a big thing of my awful billets and my search, thus far unsuccessful, for a furnished apartment. "You have to get on a list for government quarters here in Salzburg, and married couples, who get preferred treatment, have to wait up to nine months."

Karl turned to his wife and winked. "I don't know if our apartment would be adequate, but we're vacating it next week because I've been transferred to Munich."

"When could I see it?" I was eager, and didn't try to hide it.

"Tonight, if you like. We'll take you out to Parsch in our car."

It was a short ride to the outskirts of Salzburg to the main gate to a crowded displaced persons camp. Across

192

the street, opposite the gate was a tree-lined long driveway leading up to a magnificent old timbered four-story house. Karl pointed up to a large stone plaque high above the front door. A life-sized bas-relief of a man in hunting clothes looked down on us.

"That's Saint Hubert, patron saint of hunters." His wife added, "Welcome to Villa Hubertus!"

I was overwhelmed by the dignity and the beauty of the house, and unprepared for the grandeur of the rooms inside and the nineteenth century furnishings. I gulped. (This place must cost a fortune to rent!) "Karl, may I ask how much the owners would be asking for rent?"

"It sounds like a lot in Schillings, so I'll tell you in dollars. Ninety-six dollars a month, and that includes all utilities, linen and towel service, and a once-a-week *Putz-frau* (cleaning woman)."

(That's about 25% of my month's pay, but it's worth every penny of it!) I was thrilled to have such a comfortable, elegant place of my own. The walls were covered with little wooden plaques on which antlers were mounted, each bearing an inscription telling the date and place of the antlers' owner's demise, and seemingly countless small paintings. Over the fireplace in the forty-foot square walnut panelled living-room hung an oil portrait of a seventeenth century gentleman proudly holding a dead rabbit in his gloved hands. The master bedroom was so big, two oversized armoires and a concert grand piano fit nicely, with room for a pair of easy chairs and a table in front of a double bed.

The next day my friends introduced me to the landlord and his wife, a cultured couple who spoke quite fluent English, except they both, when I thanked them for some accommodation they had granted, would reply, "Oh, do not mention IT!"

I moved in the next day, and spent an hour photographing the house, inside and out. I was anxious for my mother to see how her son, the intelligence officer was living. I dashed down to the Army Special Services darkroom in downtown Salzburg. Its wall adjoined the Mozarteum, a renowned school of music. As I developed my negatives, I could hear through the walls a soprano repeating her scales over and over, and her teacher pounding the top of a piano, shouting at her. It reminded me of my old violin teacher back in Oshkosh, who pounded his fist into the wall and swore at me in German whenever I played a sour note.

I made a point of keeping my 'digs' *top secret*, not wanting to incur resentment and envy, particularly anong the higher officers in my unit. (My C.O. and his wife were living in a tiny apartment above an *Apoteke* (pharmacy) nearby.) Once settled in at Villa Hubertus, I got into the pleasant habit of stopping at Tomaselli Café for breakfast on my way to my office at Lehener Kaserne, on the other side of the city.

Tomaselli's was one of Salzburg's most popular coffee houses, a meeting place for locals during the off-season. During the tourist season it was practically taken over by tourists with their cameras, guidebooks and postcards. Its nineteenth century charm returned with the advent of cool weather, and back came the quiet, well-dressed Salzburgers, reading their newspapers on sticks, sipping expresso and making up for all the pastries they had done without during the war.

~~~

39.

The Austrians Through Our Eyes 1952

It seemed to my fellow officers and me, when we first arrived in Austria, that we would never get used to the Austrian habit of staring at us. Evidently it was not in their culture to regard staring as impolite. On the whole, despite this one frequent lapse, we found most Austrians affable and extremely polite in their dealings with us.

Another facet that disturbed us was their seeming accident-proneness. For example, one morning a heavy-set Austrian workman came into my office to install a new lighting fixture in the ceiling. He brought with him what looked like a homemade ladder, with such thin rungs that they might bear the weight of a ten year-old child. I sensed disaster in the making as he began his ascent up the ladder. Not bearing to watch, I turned all my attention to a report I was typing. A loud series of cracking sounds ended with a stupendous thump, as the workman's knees broke the ladder's rungs from halfway up. Landing on the floor, he shouted a resounding "*Scheiss!*" The Austrian equivalent of the ubiquitous French expletive, "*Merde!*"

During the winter months, icy streets didn't deter Salzburgers from riding their bicycles, and at one particular intersection where train tracks turned east toward the suburb of Parsch, as I would return to Villa Hubertus at the end of the day it was heart-wrenching to see one bicyclist after another get their bike's wheels caught in the icy tracks, to be thrown unto the pavement.

One Sunday afternoon I witnessed a dedication ceremony commemorating the restoration of a church bell in a village church outside Salzburg. During the war many church bells had been confiscated by the Nazis to be melted down for armaments. Firemen had set up a block and tackle rig to hoist a heavy new bell into the church tower. As they teamed up to pull the rope, the bell slowly rose from the ground, and the crowd of spectators began applauding. Suddenly a loud "ping" echoed against the walls of nearby buildings. An iron retaining pin which had been driven into the tower wall to hold fast a pulley flew through the air like a bullet, striking a young boy in the head. He died instantly.

~~~

40.
Cold War R&R - 1953

M y unit, in its wisdom, decided that whenever pos sible, compensatory time off for remaining on duty more than fifty hours a week should be dispensed to relieve the tedium of report writing and the stresses of living and working in KGB-infested areas throughout our American Zone in Austria. One of my fellow intelligence officers took advantage of Rest and Recreation time off to risk travelling through the Soviet Zone from our intelligence complex in Linz to Vienna, driving through the Soviet check point on the Inn River, and being followed by suspicious Red Army patrols while enroute to Vienna. On the American check point at the Inn River we had to phone in our location and exact time that we would be crossing into the Soviet Zone to our headquarters in Vienna. If we arrived in Vienna too soon, we would be fined for speeding through the Soviet Zone. If we failed to show up at the American checkpoint in Vienna in a reasonable amount of time, our authorities would assume we were being detained by the Russians, not a pretty prospect.

Why all this devotion to Vienna? Bob Donnelly was an avid collector of swords, knights' armour, African spears and shields, all of which he figured would someday provide him with a good living in a shop of his own in Washington, D.C., his hometown. Once in Vienna he would go directly to a nationally-run pawnshop, the Dorotheum, a former convent of four floors full of jewelry, furniture, musical instruments, objects d ' art, medieval weapons and armour, and African weaponry. He would spend hours in the *Aktionsalle* (auction hall) bidding on spears and swords, helmets and shields. I accompanied him on several of his R&R's to Vienna, and when we both had to board a crowded tram carrying his menacing acquisitions of spears and shields, we provoked anxious stares from our fellow passengers. Upon arrival at the Bristol Hotel lobby, the staff and the bell man, accustomed to seeing Bob Donnelly laden with antique weapons, would good-naturedly carry his booty up to his room.

On the outskirts of Salzburg standing amid well-landscaped grounds was Schloss Klessheim, a Versailles-styled small palace. After the *Anschluss,* Hitler requisitioned the palace as a rest and relaxation center for his top generals and field marshals. Its elegant interior was decorated with large, impressive tapestries and vases filled with fresh-cut flowers. But in 1952, any Nazi bigwigs who survived the war no longer were welcome at Schloss Klessheim.

The U.S. Army took over the palace after the war and turned it into a sparkling, luxurious officers' club, complete with hotel rooms for visiting guests. When the rooms were cleaned and accessorized for occupancy it was discovered that every one of the palace's rooms was "bugged." Not even Hitler's closest military leaders were above suspicion.

Once or twice a week in the evenings our intelligence unit's officers and wives would meet there for dinner and a rather unurbane bingo game. Merchandise prizes from the local Army Post Exchange consisted mainly of household appliances, cash prizes and Austrian-made glass-domed clocks with three-balled pendulums that swung back and forth for eight days without rewinding. The three balls reminded me of the three brass balls I saw at New York and Chicago pawn shops.

Cold War R&R - 1953

Speaking of pawn shops, in Austria, there were no privately-owned pawn shops as we knew them back in the States: seedy, tawdry-looking establishments that always featured guns, tools and guitars in their windows. In Austria, several of its larger cities offered instead large, government-run *"Dorotheums,"* bulging with objets d' art, high quality furniture, antiques, jewels, musical instruments of every description, and swords and armor. Lab-coated civil service employees ran these pawnshops with the efficiency and tidiness seen only in the better hospitals of the country. I say "better," because on one occasion, when I had to take an employee to a local Salzburg hospital, I was appalled to see birds flying through the corridors, and nurses wearing dirty, bloodstained aprons, some with cigarettes dangling from their mouths, taking blood samples from patients.

Another friend in the unit, Joe Sherman, and I would take an afternoon off once a month to drive to a small town west of Linz called Wels. Our R&R consisted of going to Austrian government-owned stables where many of their world-renowned Lipizzaner stallions were cared for by patient, perserverent trainers. The stables looked as if they harked back to the days of the Austro-Hungarian Empire. The horses seemed to me to be statuary in motion. They had been saved from the Soviets during the closing days of the war by a special task force set up by General Patton, taking them out of Czechoslovakia and returning them to the American Zone in Austria. Thanks to General Patton, the world's horse lovers can now go to Vienna instead of to Moscow to watch their elegant performances.

The *Salzkammergut* (lake district), east of Salzburg) drew us like a magnet with its serene, idyllic atmosphere. Our intelligence unit had several cottages along its lakes where we brought selected high-profile German and Austrian prisoners of war who were finally released from Soviet Labor camps, shipyards and factories after years of incarceration and exploitation by their Soviet keepers. The cottages became "debriefing" (a euphemism for "interrogation") centers, where our intelligence people would glean as much detailed information about potential Soviet targets as possible, and forward it to our analysts to be collated and evaluated, and finally to be distributed to those with a "need to know."

Along the shore of one of the lakes was a small castle named "Schloss Fuschel," the former home of Nazi Foreign Minister Von Ribbentrop. By 1952 it had been converted into an R&R destination for American Officers. It had a superb dining room, and its comfortable chalet-style cottages within its complex afforded a complete respite from the strains and stresses of intelligence collecting.

Thirty years later I took Nancy to dinner at Schloss Fuschel, now a privately owned hotel. The head waiter, remembering my face from my frequent visits back in 1953 and 1954, assumed that by now I must be at least a full colonel, and addressed me as "*Herr Oberst,*" accompanying his greeting with a click of his heels and a deferential nod of his head.

(Unlike the Germans, Austrians for the most part regarded us as liberators rather than conquerors, so our presence in Austria was not resented or resisted.)

~~~

41.

A Brush with the KGB 1953

In 1953 my intelligence unit was running a school for intelligence specialists at Linz, on the Danube, halfway between Salzburg and Vienna. Linz was an industrial town, home of the former Herman Goering Steel Works, and could lay claim to having had Adolph Hitler as a one-time resident. Across the Danube, at Urfahr, the Soviets had military units, whose size, mission, and state of preparedness intrigued us as much as our forces on the Linz side intrigued them. Our Russian neighbors regularly sent over the bridge numerous low-grade, low-paid Austrian agents to keep tab on our goings and comings, particularly at the Hotel Linzerhof, our American officers' hotel right on the bank of the Danube.

My first night in Linz I was assigned a room from which I could see the red Soviet flag and sentries on the other side of the bridge checking the papers of everyone crossing the bridge. The Linzerhof's parking lot proved to be a popular training ground for Soviet agents. They would loiter around the entrance, wearing long leather coats and tyrolean hats, looking as if they had been selected by some Hollywood casting director. When an American car drew up to the entrance, they would whip out little notebooks and jot down the car's license plate numbers. They knew, and couldn't care less that we were aware of their activities. On one occasion, I decided to make a joke of their amateurish spying efforts. One rainy day, at the entrance to the parking lot, I got out of my car and wiped off the mud on my license plates so that they could more easily read the numbers. They failed to see the humor, and showed no appreciation whatsoever.

After the first few nights at the Linzerhof, the novelty of sleeping in a bed just a hundred yards away from our cold war adversaries wore off, and I was able to sleep much more soundly.

I spent the first few days in Linz boning up on my O.B. (*Order of Battle*) course I was preparing to teach at the United States Forces Austria's Intelligence School. As an *O.B.* specialist, I was keen to know as much as possible about the Soviet armed forces across the river, their composition, state of training and particularly about the arrival and departure of Soviet units in the area.

As part of my unit's "Blue Plate Special," all newly arrived intelligence officers were given a week to tour our far-flung units and detachments, to get an overall view of our mission and operations in Austria. On my trip to Vienna, I found that I had an hour before I was to attend a briefing. I decided to walk from my hotel, the Bristol, to an outdoor café on the Schottenring, one of Vienna's busiest boulevards. On the way, I had to pass the entrance of the Soviet Army's officer's hotel, formerly known as the Grand Hotel. My approach to their hotel was blocked by two large, heavy saw-horses, which obliged all of us pedestrians to pass the entrance out on the street. Looking toward the entrance, I saw two guards with *Pe-pe-sha's* (Russian submachine guns) checking the I.D.'s of every officer entering the hotel. Through big plate glass windows backed by a heavy iron mesh screen, you could make out Soviet officers smoking their long cigarettes and drinking.

What a contrast! I thought. At the Bristol, there are no guards, no barriers, no mesh screens, no-one to check you as you enter. Ironic, isn't it? The Soviets spend huge amounts on putting on fancy, impressive parades and military displays to impress and to intimidate us, but at the same time openly acknowledge to the world their paranoia and unpopularity by turning their officers' hotel into a fortress, just yards away from our own wide-open hotel, the Bristol!"

I found an outdoor café on the Ringstrasse, and sat down at a table facing a busy intersection. Since I was in the International Sector of Vienna, I could see soldiers of the four occupying powers and Viennese enjoying the crisp autumn air. I was sipping coffee, wearing civilian clothes, topped by a Tyrolean hat complete with a chamois "brush," and snugly insulated against the cold by a poplin lined dark brown corduroy topcoat. I could have passed for a well-heeled Viennese enjoying a lunch break.

At the intersection's pedestrian crossing stood a knot of bandy-legged Soviet Uzbeck soldiers wearing on their shoulderboards an insignia I had never before seen in my Soviet O.B. files and charts. Just as a philatalist having spotted a never before catalogued stamp, I wanted to make a record of that unique, strange-looking insignia.

I set my Rolleiflex camera on the table, aimed it at the middle of the intersection and prefocused it so that when the soldiers were just ten feet from my table the camera's self-timer would trip the shutter. It was a way of taking photos without being noticed raising the camera to my eye, or touching the shutter release.

As I was surreptitiously operating my camera, a small, bug-like black Czech-made Tatra stopped in the middle of the intersection. Even though it was jamming up traffic on all sides, the Austrian policeman directing traffic, typically impatient and irritable on such an occasion, seemed to be pretending that the Tatra wasn't there. I looked into the dark interior of the car, some fifty feet ahead, and caught the glint of a pair of binoculars pointing right at me! A sudden chill coursed up my spine. *(They're onto me! That cop is ignoring them because he's afraid! They're KGB! I'd better go into the café, and beat it out the back door, before they nab me right here on the street!)* As I dashed down a dark corridor and passed the kitchen, the face of a hometown clairvoyant, Mrs. LeDoit, flashed before my eyes. Ten years before, she had answered my questions about a terrifying dream I had of being lined up against a wall and shot by a firing squad. She was shaking her finger at me. "Jack, so long as you don't go 'round stickin' yore nose in other folks' business, you'll live to be an old man. It's a kinda warnin'."

Headed toward the back door, I took off my glasses, took off my topcoat, slung my camera by its strap over my shoulder, and turned my coat inside out so that the light poplin side showed. Then I remembered my hat. (My *Tyroler Hut*! It'll be a dead giveaway!) Near the end of the corridor I spotted a wall-mounted steam radiator, mashed up my hat and jammed it between the radiator and the wall.

As I left by way of the rear exit door, I saw the left front fender of that black Tatra, its front wheel up on the curb and its motor running. My heart was pounding as I thought, *(The KGB's motto is "Smersh Spionom" - "Death to Spies"). "Calm, John, calm. Walk slowly past that car and don't look at them!"* I turned left out of the door, my hands clasped behind my back, Austrian-style. It worked! Reversing my coat, hiding my camera and getting rid of my my hat had thrown them off the scent. As I distanced myself from their car I quickened my pace. A short block away was my hotel, the Bristol. Once I got inside, they wouldn't dare to follow me in - or would they! By now I was sweating and shaking. Entering the lobby, I now wished they had some kind of guard at the door, to keep them from following me in. I dared not look back, but headed for the back of the lobby, where I saw a barbershop sign. Not waiting to be asked to be seated, I bolted into the barber chair and ordered, "Towels on my face! Schnell!"

It was an hour later that I ventured out of the hotel. I made a point from then on never to wear that coat again in Vienna, and to forsake forever wearing a *Tyroler hut*.

I turned up at the briefing very late, and felt I owed the briefing officer an explanation.

"Sorry I missed so much of the briefing. I got held up by a traffic jam on the Ringstrasse."

~~~

42.

And The Flag Was Still There - 1954

There stands in a former monastery courtyard in Vienna one of the world's unloveliest towers. During the Second World War the German Army constructed that squat, reinforced concrete tower, bristled it at the top with anti-aircraft guns to defend Vienna from allied bombing attacks. A grim and ugly reminder of a half-century-old fact, it still stands in a city renowned for its architectural beauty. It's just too difficult and expensive to demolish, so Vienna will be stuck with it for many more years to come.

Despite its grim history, I have a particular fondness for "Der Flakturm Stiftskaserne" (Flak Tower of the Monastery Garrison). Back in the nineteen fifties, the Stiftskaserne was an American Army Constabulary Headquarters, during an era of chilly Cold War relations with our Soviet counterparts in Vienna. The Soviet side was growing more petulant and obstructive daily.

One side of the tower faced the Soviet-held sector of Vienna. Our U.S. Army commander had a large American flag composed of over a hundred red, white and blue light-bulbs installed at the uppermost section of the tower facing the Soviet Sector. "A beacon of freedom" it was called, intended to beckon, to lure Soviet defectors to the West. The Soviet authorities, annoyed and embarrassed by that visual thorn in their side, decided that the flag must go, one way or another. After vain complaints to the American commander, his Russian counterpart threatened to "do something" about that flag. But the flag was still there, night after night, shining its beguiling message into the Russian Sector. Even resorting to a sharpshooter up in a church tower in the Russian Zone only temporarily dimmed the flag. Every morning a detail of military policemen had to climb up the side of the tower and replace the broken bulbs.

And the flag did its work. One snowy February night in 1953, an officer of the USSR's dreaded secret police apparatus, KGB Major Piotr Deriabin turned himself in at the Stiftskaserne, seeking asylum in the United States. It so happened that Deriabin was in charge of a program to keep KGB agents from defecting to the West, extremely knowledgeable about the KGB's anti-defection policies and activities. He had been sent to Vienna to nip any attempted defections in the bud. A most valuable acquisition for the CIA, he had to be spirited out of Vienna, and quickly, for Vienna was infested with KGB agents and paid informers.

Getting the Red Out

Our intelligence people were faced with a difficult problem: how to get him out safely and quickly.

All roads out of Vienna were patrolled by Soviet troops, Vienna's railway stations were swarming with KGB people, and the air terminal was closely watched day and night since Deriabin's disappearance. We would have flown him out from our small airstrip in the American Zone, but heavy snows ruled that out. It was decided that our American passenger train, The Mozart would be used to get our "red bird" out, even though it meant traversing almost a hundred kilometers of Soviet-held territory with a twenty-minute stop for inspection at their garrison town of Amstettin. In Soviet minds, the Mozart would be our least likely option, for every passenger would be checked and re-checked, and the train's undercarriage would be thoroughly inspected at every stop. That gave us a window of opportunity: to get Deriabin on the train not as a passenger, but disguised as freight to be loaded in the baggage car. The next problem to be solved was, what kind of freight?

Our "red bird" was encased in a large hot water tank, part of a shipment of hot water tanks consigned to a plumber's shop in Salzburg, in the American Zone. Air holes had been inconspicuously drilled into the underside of the tank and the end of the tank had been welded shut. A large hand-drawn baggage wagon was pulled by porters down the long ramp to the Mozart's baggage car, past the noses of the KGB. At the same time, as a distraction, several Deriabin look-a-likes were sent to board the train and to be nabbed, and detained for questioning, only to be released when confronted by some of Deriabin's colleagues. The ruse worked, and our "red bird" was on his way to Washington, courtesy of the CIA.

A couple of months after Deriabin's escape, I had lunch with an old friend, Lt. Colonel Oaks, who was the U.S. Army's Provost Marshal in Vienna, in command of the U.S. Constabulary stationed at the Stiftskaserne. The colonel was in a buoyant mood.

"The Russkies about a month ago, in retaliation for the defection of Deriabin, stepped up their sniping at our electric flag until every night more and more lights were shot out. During our monthly meeting, I warned the Soviet Provost Marshal that the sniping must stop, or he would have reason to regret it. The Russian laughed just as he had before, and again claimed that it must be an Austrian doing the shooting. The nightly sniping continued. I requested that the Department of the Army find the tallest officer in the U.S. Army, and send him to Vienna for a few days. They sent me a captain, six feet seven inches tall. We put him into a military police officer's uniform, and made him commander of our guard that took part in a formal Changing of the Guard ceremony in Vienna's International Zone, marking the assumption for the following month of control of the International Zone by the Soviets. The monthly Change of the Guard ceremony took place in a big city square witnessed by crowds of Viennese. To symbolize U.S. - U.S.S.R. cooperation, such as it was, each country's military band played its respective national anthem. Then the two Guard commanders, U.S. and Russian, marched into the center of the square, to salute each other and to shake hands. But on this occasion, the Soviet Guard officer, who was barely five feet five inches tall, had practically to stand on tiptoes in order to shake hands with the American giant. The crowd roared with laughter and jeers. After that little episode, the sniping stopped."

And so the flag was still there. I've seen many towers: The Tower of Pisa, The Eiffel Tower, the tower at Fréjus, in southern France where Spanish soldier-poet Garcilasco de la Vega was struck on the head by a boulder sent down from the top of the tower by French peasants defending their homeland; San Francisco's Coit Tower, which withstood the 'quake of 1989; and last but not least, Oshkosh's own nearly two hundred foot steel water tower which as a young boy I watched as the rivetters made it rise from the ground as if it were made from a giant erector set. But there is one tower that stands above all others, so to speak, in my mind, anyway: The Flakturm in Vienna's Stiftskaserne.

The M.P.'s who had to climb the Flakturm every morning to replace all those broken red, white and blue bulbs would have inspired another Frances Scott Keye had there been one present. Their grandchildren by now will have heard how they made sure that the flag was still there.

~~~

My post-war intelligence service in London, Paris and Central Europe provided me with an essential "tool of my trade" a camera. The following articles tell about adventures and misadventures, some of which were due to my love of photography, and my post-war civilian life as a professional photographer in Carmel, California.

43.

Trophy Shooting in Spain - 1967

While travelling, I'm always on the lookout for another "shooting" trophy to hang on my wall back home. Unlike big game hunters, however, my weapon of choice isn't a rifle, but a camera. My trophies, well, they aren't three-dimensional and stuffed, but two-dimensional, matted and framed. As in hunting big game, the more elusive and difficult the prey, the more prized the trophy.

I had my heart set on "shooting" a Spanish Civil Guard in all his inbred aloofness and brusqueness, symbolic of Generalissimo Francisco Franco's fascist dictatorship, and I soon found that would not be easy, despite the fact that everywhere you go in Spain, you're bound to see them, patrolling in pairs, their black patent leather three-cornered hats glistening in the sun, their faces tanned and deeply lined by the elements, the corners of their mouths evincing an immutable scowl. A much desired addition to my collection of trophies, but practically unattainable; forbidden fruit.

My "Rollei," unlike most other cameras, could be aimed from waist level, not raised to the eye, so a "sneak" shot, unnoticed by my quarry, was statistically, at least, more likely of success than with an eye-level camera. But after several abortive attempts, after having been rudely shouted at in staccato-like Spanish, *"No! Está prohibido! Ni una fotografía siquiera!"* (No! It's prohibited! Not even one photo!") I began to wonder if it was worth the effort.

One hot day at Palma, Mallorca Airport, my wife Nancy and our daughter Terry were standing on the tarmac, waiting for me to join them and board the plane for Barcelona. I had gone to the Customs office to retrieve a box containing a new Rollei Camera and a slide projector I had bought a few weeks before in Switzerland. Customs officers the world over seem to develop a sixth sense, and can almost smell a potential smuggler. The Palma Customs officer, seemingly endowed with a hyper-sensitivity which tripped alarm bells in his head as soon as he saw me, earlier had impounded my heavy, suspicious-looking box to preclude my selling my photographic arsenal during my stay in Mallorca, with the understanding that it would be returned to me upon my departure from Palma.

Carrying the box out of his office and through the exit door from the waiting room, as soon as I was outside, two burly Civil Guards; their tunics buttoned up to their sweaty throats and their oily sub-machine guns hanging from their shoulder straps, formed an escort around me, one at each of my elbows, and marched me past my alarmed wife and daughter up the ramp and into the plane. They weren't about to countenance my selling my photographic equipment anywhere between the waiting room exit door and the door of the plane. Once on board, they saw to it that my box had been stowed in the compartment above my seat, and then left the plane without a word.

My wife and daughter finally joined me aboard, they along with fellow passengers, had received the distinct impression that I had been arrested, and was being escorted by the Guardias for trial on the mainland. It took a while to regain their composure.

This wasn't the first or the last brush I'd had with El Caudillo Franco's *Guardia Civil*, but I was determined not to leave Spain without at least one good "shot" of one of these stern, no-nonsense enforcers of Franco's edicts.

The Guardia Civil was around long before Franco seized power. They were established as an elite paramilitary police force in 1844, and have had a well-earned reputation for severity and even brutality when the occasion arises. Somehow, under the broiling Mallorcan sun, the idea had not come to me to "shoot" my escorts. Perhaps on the mainland I'd have better opportunities.

Once we settled in our hotel suite in Barcelona, we heard beautiful strains of Chopin coming from the suite below. What a welcome contrast to the taped concert of off-key Sinatra vocals our cab driver had treated us to all the way from the airport! During a lull in the Chopin music, I was tempted to pound on the floor in an effort to get the pianist started up again, but it would probably have been misconstrued.

Later that afternoon we went down to the lobby for tea. As we sat down we noticed a familiar-looking elderly gentleman having an earnest conversation with a beautiful, statuesque blonde, probably in her early thirties. Nancy tapped my elbow and whispered, "John! Isn't that –"

"It certainly is," I interrupted. It's Artur Rubinstein!" That explains the beautiful Chopin we heard upstairs. His suite must be directly beneath ours."

Nancy was excited. "Go over there and ask him if he remembers meeting you at the party the Army Language School gave him while you were studying Polish there."

"But Nancy dear, that was 'way back in 1952. He may not remember me, and besides, he wouldn't appreciate my breaking into his tète à tète with that Lorelei."

We sat there for a good half-hour, waiting for an opportunity to talk to the Maestro. At long last, as the couple rose from their chairs about to leave, I walked up to them and said in my best Polish, *"Przepraszam, pana. Czy pan pamienta Wojskowa Szkole Jezyków w Monterey?"* (Excuse me, sir. Do you remember the Army Language School in Monterey?")

Rubinstein, surprised and delighted to be addressed in his native language, offered his hand, which I shook very gingerly, mindful of my usual habit of proffering a strong, hearty handshake, something my father had drilled into me when I was a small boy. "None of that limp fish stuff," he would tell me. But those hands, I thought, must be insured for millions of dollars, so it turned out to be a rather limp handshake.

Rubinstein thought for a moment about what I had asked him. "Tak jest! To sie stalo w Club Oficerski, w ´srodku pola karczochów!" (Yes indeed! That took place at the Officers' Club in the middle of an artichoke field!")

"Almost, but not quite," I replied as tactfully as I could, for the nearest artichoke field was some ten miles away from the Presidio of Monterey's Officers' Club.

Rubinstein said, "You must be of Polish descent, to speak Polish so well."

My repertoire of Polish phrases on the verge of exhaustion, I replied in English, "Thank you for the compliment, but no, there's not a drop of Polish blood in me, unfortunately. It was because I had great teachers while at the school, that I learned enough to get by." I lapsed back into Polish once more as my wife approached.

"Moja zona, Nancy." (My wife, Nancy.)

Rubinstein arose and gave a courtly nod and said in English, "A great pleasure, madame." Nancy and I both noticed that he studiously avoided bringing his blonde friend into the conversation. As they walked toward the elevator, in my mind's eye I saw his portrait among my trophies on my wall. I asked, "Mr. Rubinstein, would you allow me to take your picture right here in the foyer?"

"Why not? But of course," he graciously replied, turning his best side to the camera and lifting his chin, anticipating what I would have asked for. After taking one picture, I felt I might be slighting his lady friend if I didn't at least offer to take her picture alongside him. As I was about to ask her, the old gentleman winked at me, and turned his thumb down in an emphatic no configuration that left no doubt that neither the National Enquirer nor anyone else was to ever have access to such a picture. As the couple stood waiting for the elevator door to separate us forever, they good-naturedly waved good-bye to us as if we were seeing them off on the Queen Elizabeth.

A few days later in Madrid, that old lusting for a photo of a Civil Guard resurfaced; I just had to have one for my trophy wall, a portrait that would capture the cold, severe demeanor of one of these creatures. I made several attempts, but always the same rebuff: "No! Está prohibido!"

I decided to go to the Headquarters of the Guardia Civil in Madrid, to see the Director General, himself, if necessary to obtain written authorization, a *Permiso* to "shoot" a Civil Guard.

The Comandante of the Guardia Civil was a short, stocky man. I'm below average height, but I seemed to tower over him. (Tiny, just like Franco), I thought. (In Spain high rank seems to be in inverse proportion to physical height). When I had finished explaining the purpose of my visit and telling him that someday I hoped to do a pictorial book on Spain, and that no such book would be complete without a good photo of one of his Civil Guards, "so much a part of Spanish life and history," the Comandante mulled it over for a minute. Then he looked me straight in the eye and asked, "Do you give me your word of honer that any pictures you take of the Guardia Civil will portray them in a good light, that no picture will create any embarrassment for our proud Corps?"

"Yes, sir, you have my word. I will show them how they are, proud, brave and loyal."

Satisfied with my response, he said, touching his chest, "I feel deep in my heart that you are a man of honor, and that you will keep your word. I therefore will authorize a *Permiso* to be prepared and issued to you."

Thanking him profusely, I felt like a knight thanking King Arthur for having been granted a munificent boon.

Trophy Shooting in Spain - 1967

The Comandante sent me down a corridor with a note to his Press Officer, which instructed him to draw up the necessary document. I spent the better part of an hour twiddling my thumbs in his outer office, gazing at a romanticized, soft-focus photograph of Civil Guards stereotypically grim-faced, marching ten abreast down a wide street, trying to keep control over ten ferocious-looking police dogs, their fangs bared, straining at their chain leashes.

The Press Officer, emerging from his office with a diploma-looking document in hand, noticed my interest in the picture.

"Un desfile reciente," (A recent parade), he informed me, his voice tinged with pride.

The next day, armed with an impressive document complete with an embossed red seal and duly rubber-stamped, my wife, daughter and I set out in a rented car for La Mancha, an arid, hot rural area south of Madrid. It was there I would put my *Permiso* to the test. With such a *Permiso*, no Guardia Civil would dare to stop me in my quest.

As we drove into a small tumble-down town I spotted a lone Guardia Civil leaning against a wall of a house, talking to an unkempt-looking woman who was sitting in her window. Civil Guards are indoctrinated to remain aloof and not to fraternize with the locals, so I deduced that the woman must be his wife. I left the car, approached him, armed with my Rollei and my *Permiso*. I handed the document to him, and told him in no uncertain Spanish that the Director General Himself had authorized me to take *his* picture. The woman, on hearing this, cackled, "Why the devil do you want to take his picture? He's *so* ugly!" Now I was certain she was his wife. He ignored the insult, examined the Permiso for a few seconds while holding it upside down. He was either

illiterate or had very weak eyes, I thought. Then he handed it
back to me, and ordered me to read it aloud to him. As soon
as I had finished reading the formal, official bureaucratese-
studded language to him, his whole attitude and demeanor
changed from stern to simpering, almost angelic, anxious to
please. As I pointed my camera at him, he produced a faint
smile, bringing into play facial muscles which had atrophied
long ago.

I was unhappy with the photo. Mission
unaccomplished. The Guardia had been intimidated by the
Permiso, and the resultant photo was a far cry from what I
had wanted to capture on film, a prototypical tough, hard-
bitten, menacing Guardia Civil.

I recalled that a famed French photographer, Henri
Cartier-Bresson years before had produced a never-to-be
equalled portrait of a brutal looking Guardia Civil. My
photo couldn't hold a candle to it. Perhaps I wasn't meant to
shoot Civil Guards, I told myself.

On second thought, having a picture of a benign-
looking, kindly Civil Guard would certainly be considered
a rarity. I hadn't realized until much later that I had a truly
one-of-a-kind, unique trophy.

The French have an apt saying for this: "Tant pis,
tant mieux." (So much the worse, so much the better.)

~~~

44.

Mein Feind, Mein Freund - 1996 (My Enemy, My Friend)

Nancy and I recently received an invitation to a birthday party, an invitation we hated to decline, because the "birthday boy" was one of our dearest friends. Actually, he wasn't really a "boy" anymore. Our friend Dieter Braun had just turned seventy. There were reasons we couldn't attend. The birthday party was to take place in Vienna, and we had too many commitments here in Carmel.

Let me tell you about Dieter Braun. About fifteen years ago Nancy and I met by chance Dieter and his wife Renate in a local restaurant. They were visiting the U.S. for the first time, and were particularly smitten with Carmel. Something happened that rarely takes place between total strangers, especially foreigners. We all felt a strong mutual respect and attraction for one another. Perhaps it was because I had known Vienna well, having lived and worked near Vienna during the Cold War Years. But it was far more than that. During our first conversation we discovered that we, Dieter and I, shared a fateful "synchronism," for want of a better term. During the first week in March, 1945, we both had been soldiers in the very same battle sector near Cologne, along the Rhine River. But there was one major difference: Dieter was a German soldier and I was an American G.I.. At that time I was manning an observation post for an artillery unit, and it was my "duty" to call in artillery fire on any German target I could spot through my binoculars. If I had caught a glimpse of Dieter, my enemy at any time during those horrendous days of collective insanity, I would have felt no compunction to zero in a rain of high explosives on my enemy, even with a feeling of elation. It was the *Zeitgeist* of the times: kill or be killed.

The loss of eighteen-year-old Dieter Braun would have been not only a tragedy for him and his family, but for the world, and for me. The world would never have known his rollicking sense of humor, his kindness, his effervescence. Neither would I.

A couple of years after our initial meeting in Carmel, Dieter, his wife and two children came back to Carmel for a short visit, and we renewed our friendship enjoying every moment of their visit, sharing the beauty of this area with them.

In November, 1988 Nancy and I checked in at Salzburg's "O.H." Hotel (Oesterreichicherhof), our first visit to Austria in many years. When it was an Army officer's hotel back in the 'fifties we found it more convenient to refer to it as the "O.H.." I mentioned to the bellman that I had frequently dined at the "O.H." while I was stationed in Salzburg. His face lit up, and smiling broadly, he exclaimed, "I never forget a face! I remember you! When I was ten years old, you and your men came to our orphanage at Christmas time and brought gifts and candy!"

That bellman couldn't do enough for us from that moment on.

We called Dieter in Vienna and told him we were spending the night at the O.H. and would arrive in Vienna the next day by train.

"No you won't!" He shouted. Renate and I will drive to Salzburg and meet you at the hotel tonight. We'll stay overnight at the hotel, have breakfast with you, and take you in our car to Vienna."

When the Brauns arrived, they noticed how attentive, almost fawning, the bellman was toward us. Dieter quipped, "What did you do, John, promise him a tip big enough to retire on?"

Enroute to Vienna, we stopped for lunch in the beautiful lake-studded Salzkammergut region. Dieter turned off the main highway and said, "We'll make a little detour here. We want to show you something special. You have your Carmel-by-the-Sea, and we have our Carmel-by-the-Lake!"

Our puzzlement evaporated when Dieter drove up to a lake-side yacht club. As we got out of the car, he walked ahead and stopped in front of a shrouded sailboat in dry-dock, pulled back a tarpaulin to reveal silver letters on its stern. **Carmel**, the letters proudly proclaimed. Dieter and Renate were beaming proudly, as if they had just unveiled a priceless work of art.

Closer to Vienna, we stopped at the huge Benedictine Abbey at Melk on high ground overlooking the Danube. An old friend and former Army Language School instructor of mine, Janusz Kodrebski, had spent his boyhood there as a student. Its Baroque chapel had been recently refurbished and its gold leaf encrusted interior shone like gems under a jeweler's light.

Further on, we stopped for supper at a riverside inn, famous for its regional dishes and wines. All during our delightful conversation I kept thinking how wonderful it was to share this time and place with friends who meant so much to us. How the passage of time had completely changed our attitude toward each other! How could we ever have been enemies?

Our stay in Vienna with the Brauns as our hosts was what made us realize what true friends we had become. A wonderful dinner at their home with their children, and the following evening, a "night on the town" crowned by a music-laden dinner in a Grinzing restaurant are memories we will always cherish. Dieter Braun, my former enemy, now my best friend. Who says good cannot come out of war?

~~~

45.

We Never Called Him Herbert - 1971

Detective Inspector Herbert Sheed of Scotland Yard was my friend and mentor during the autumn months of 1945.

He was an unforgettable character, not the stereotypical cop one sees time and again on television and films. He was urbane, well-spoken, and above all, always tactful and considerate even in times of great stress. We worked together on a number of cases in London, where the United States Army had assigned me as a criminal investigations agent.

When I moved my family to the United Kingdom some twenty-five years later, the first thing I did when we arrived in London was to dart across the street from our hotel to the new Scotland Yard headquarters, while the rest of my family slumbered off the effects of jet lag. Mr. Sheed, though we were on friendly terms, never called me anything but "Livingstone" or "Livingstone, old chap," even though he was at least thirty years my senior. And naturally, I always called him Mr. Sheed, instinctively feeling he would never brook being called by his first name. That might have happened in California, but not in the United Kingdom.

I asked a uniformed constable at the reception desk, "Would you please give me the phone number and address of Detective Inspector Sheed?"

The constable peered at me over his half-glasses with a look of absolute incredulity, as if I were asking for complimentary tickets to the Queen's coronation. He turned to a large file on a table behind him.

"Sheed, Detective Inspector Sheeds. Ah, there we are. Well, sir, 'e's retired and not on our active list. I expect 'e's still knocking about, but I'm not allowed to give out 'is 'phone number or 'is address. "Yard policy, don't you know. All we can do is give 'im your 'phone number, and the rest is up to 'im."

A week went by, and in the meantime we rented a house in a small stately suburb about twenty miles southwest of London, at Esher, Surrey. Our daughters were enrolled in a private school there in the middle of what Londoners called the "stockbroker's belt."

Soon after moving in, our phone rang. A crisp, cultivated voice greeted me. "Sheed here.. Is that you, Livingstone, old chap?" And a little reproachfully, "I've been thinking you had dropped off the face of the earth, not having heard from you for so long. . .this is the chap from Hopscotch, Isn't it?"

"Oshkosh, Mr. Sheed. Remember the last time we had a pub lunch together? It was in November, 1945. I had just received my orders transferring me to the Paris Criminal Investigation Division. You gave me that wonderful book, *"In Quest of Justice"* as a farewell present. It would be great to see you again after all these years. May we meet soon?"

"The sooner the better, old chap. What about next Monday? Ten a.m. on the south side of Nelson's Column, Trafalgar Square."

I knew I wouldn't have any difficulty spotting Mr. Sheed. He was tall, sported a neatly trimmed silver mustache, always wore a British warm coat and a bowler hat, and never went anywhere without an umbrella. My eagerly awaited meeting with Mr. Sheed took place at precisely the appointed time and place. Actually, I arrived purposely ten minutes early, and seeing him also arriving on the scene early as well, I shadowed him around the square while he searched the crowd for me. I was determined to impress him with my punctuality, to walk up to him at the exact minute we had agreed upon. Perhaps he once had a sixth sense about being followed. But being retired from police work so many years had dulled those extra-sensory powers, for he was completely unaware that I was following him closely.

Our meeting was an exuberant one, considering his usual British reserve. Retirement had mellowed him and made him more demonstrative, not that he ever lacked warmth and sincerity with friends. After having a pub lunch I invited him to come out to Esher and meet my wife the following evening. "I'll meet you at Esher Police Station," he said, "then you can take me in your car to your house."

Mr. Sheed's Weird Profession

Mr. Sheed's visit to our home was a memorable one. Nancy was captivated by this debonair, articulate man. When she asked him what he was doing to keep busy in retirement, we were both astonished and intrigued by his answer: "Oh, well, now you may think this is a bit odd, but I am making a good living *debunking spiritualists.* This work of mine keeps me hopping all over the United Kingdom and on the continent as well. You may not be aware of the fact that many elderly people are unduly influenced by "hired" spiritualists to leave their fortunes to often undeserving relatives or grasping friends. What I do is attend these seances and expose those charlatans for what they are. I'm usually hired by close relatives who feel that they will be denied their rightful inheritance by unscrupulous outsiders or family 'black sheep,' who pay these confidence tricksters to bring *spirit messages* from departed loved ones advising them to change their wills. A nasty business, that."

Mr. Sheed continued: "In one particularly amusing case, during a seance the spiritualist thought she would impress me with her genuineness: 'Mr. Sheed,' she said, 'Your mother wishes to speak to you from the other world. 'Dear Herbert, though I have been gone from your sight these many years, I still watch over you, Herbert, dear. You must know that there is really no such thing as what you call 'death.' Now, Herbert, what you have been doing these past few years disturbs me greatly. Mind what I tell you, Herbert: leave the spirit world alone; do not interfere. Now Herbert, you are nearing your seventy-fifth year. It won't be long before you join me. Do behave yourself in the meantime, Herbert. . ."

"Then the spirit voice trailed off. Of course, I didn't for one moment believe a word of that 'spirit message.' It made me laugh, and I'll tell you why. For one reason, my mother never called me Herbert; she always called me 'laddie.' Besides that, no one ever calls me by my first name more than once, even my close friends! For another reason, an hour before the seance, I left my ninety-five-year-old mother watching the telly in our flat in Hammersmith. When I mentioned these facts to the spiritualist medium, she lost her composure and stammered out something about how she had mistaken my mother for some other long-deceased Martha Sheed."

A fiction writer would be hard-pressed to conjure up a more colorful yet believable character. I've often observed that real-life people are more impressive and memorable than any writer's imagination is likely to produce.

I received a phone call recently from a total stranger who said, "Hi, John, I'm Ted. I want to share with you a real money-making idea, commodity futures..." I hung up on him. I'm sure my old friend Mr. Sheed would have preferred the London way to the California way.

~~~

46.

The Long Arm of Coincidence - 1997

One day as I walked down San Francisco's Market Street, I noticed an elderly, rumpled derelict of a man standing against a bus stop. There was something immediately, distressingly familiar about him. Although I had not set eyes on my former army colleague Joe DuMais since I left Paris for the 'States back in 1946, a weird, inexplicable series of coincidences about Joe have taunted and mystified me down through the years.

The temptation to stop and ask him, "Aren't you Joe DuMais?" was for some reason easy to resist. He had never been a friend, only a colleague. I continued on my way, having extrapolated in my mind what Joe would look like after the passage of fifty years. I was hoping against hope that the man I saw was just a mirage, or a remarkable look-alike.

We all experience what we call coincidences, most of which we attribute to or dismiss as mere chance-occurrences. But then there are those coincidences that we can't dismiss so lightly. They continue to be nagging, disquieting and worrisome throughout one's lifetime.

The strange series of coincidences involving Joe DuMais began one cold February night in a sleazy G.I. night club on the Rue Pigalle in Paris in 1946. A whole squad of U.S. military policemen poured into the "Pig Alley" nightspot, intent on "bagging" their quota of AWOLS, deserters and black marketeers for the night. The white-helmeted M.P.'s entered through the front door and began checking the G.I.'s "dog tags" and leave papers. As they progressed through the crowded, smoke-filled night club, the AWOL's and deserters among the crowd casually sidled toward the rear exit, only to be welcomed by the gaping jaws of the open twin doors of a U.S. Army paddy wagon. With a few prods by nightstick wielding M.P.'s, the miscreants found themselves jammed into the waiting "rat trap," as we called it. Once the paddy wagon was full, we took our quarry down to the M.P. booking station we shared with the Paris Prefecture Police in the basement of the Paris Opera House.

One of the suspected deserters I processed that night was a short, slender corporal of the infantry, a dishevelled, bearded G.I. in his thirties, Joe DuMais, who had no leave papers, claiming to have lost them. His hair had been dyed a reddish-orange, not even a distant match to the color of his three-or-four-day growth of beard. He claimed he had been discharged in Paris, and had re-enlisted, was finishing a month-long leave, and was to report for duty the following day with the 787th M.P. Battalion stationed in Paris. A 'phone call to the duty officer at the military police headquarters confirmed his story, and he was released with the admonishment, "you'd better report all spit and polished tomorrow or else."

A week later, Joe was assigned to me for orientation and on-the-job training in the not so genteel art of hunting and bagging AWOL's and deserters. He certainly was an unlikely looking military policeman, rather unkempt, short, and unmilitary in his demeanor, but all the more suitable for the job, since being of French-Canadian background, his Canadian-lilted French was impeccable.

Joe was not happy with the billeting situation; nor was I. Magazin Dufayel, a former department store, had been turned into a barracks by the German occupiers, and the U.S. Army inherited it for use as billets for the military police. The day-and -night ceaseless comings and goings of military policemen, their belt buckles and their night sticks constantly rattling against the cots and lockers, their raucous voices and snoring punctuated the air and left few able to get a decent night's or day's sleep. Joe invited me to share a suite of rooms at what turned out to be a fashionable, almost elegant hotel, (and it still is today), the Château Frontenac, on the Rue Pierre Charon, at no cost to me, he assured me. I immediately wondered how a corporal could afford such luxury, but I deferred until later my curiosity about his ways and means in favor of real sleep and comfortable quarters. When I arrived at the suite with my barracks bag, Joe introduced me to two other occupants of the suite, his wife, just arrived from Czechoslovakia, and her big, friendly German Shepherd dog, Azor. We must have presented a curious combination to the manager and the concièrge, this ménage à quatre.

There was something about Joe that continually gnawed at me: he was an extraordinarily quiet, private person, a man of very few words, unemotional, cold, indifferent, completely immune to the beauty and the delights of his surroundings, and indifferent, insensitive, and even careless in the performance of his investigative work. After sharing his suite for two months, I felt as if I knew even less about him then than when I first had met him in the booking station.

The Long Arm of Coincidence - 1997

The day came, in May, 1946 when I was to leave Paris and return to civilian life. Joe, his wife and I spent a rather perfunctory half-hour over a bottle of Pernod and I thanked them for their hospitality, shook hands, and left, my heavy barracks bag slung over my shoulder. We probably would never see each other again, but that was O.K. *Tant pis, tant mieux* (So much the worse, so much the better, a popular French saying).

In 1947, at the University of Wisconsin, I walked into the university's ornate Memorial Union building to have lunch. As I passed by a news-stand I caught a glimpse of a photo on the front page of the Los Angeles Times. It was a police I.D. head shot of Joe DuMais! A headline over it proclaimed, *Black Dahlia Slaying Suspect Arrested.* I bought a copy of the newspaper and immediately devoured the two-column-long article. A Captain Florence of the Army's Criminal Investigations Division was quoted as stating that Private DuMais was a prime suspect in the as yet unsolved murder of an unidentified young woman whose mutilated body was found in a vacant lot in Los Angeles. The article went on the relate DuMais was arrested during a routine barracks search for stolen property. All the soldiers were ordered to empty their pockets and turn their pockets inside out. A C.I.D. agent found what appeared to be bloodstains in one of DuMais' pockets. When tests established that the blood type was the same as the murder victim's, DuMais was placed under arrest for further investigation. *Coincidentally,* the blood type was the same as Joe's, and *coincidentally,* it was found that Joe had been on weekend pass in the Los Angeles area during the time of the murder. Under interrogation, Joe conceded that he possibly was the murderer, but that he had been on an alcoholic binge the entire time, and his memory

231

was completely blanked out. Other clues and leads failed to connect Joe with the murder, and the charges were dropped for lack of sufficient evidence.

A year later, I spotted an interesting feature article on the first page of the New York Times, a newspaper I never would have bought, but it had been abandoned on the couch alongside me. The article's continuation led me to an inside page, and having read the final words of the article, I was about to put down the paper when my eyes latched onto a small headline in an adjoining column: *Former Black Dahlia Suspect Sentenced.*

Carnival worker Joe DuMais, once a prime suspect in the Black Dahlia murder case, was sentenced to five years in Pennsylvania State Penitentiary for auto theft.

Now, this *coincidence* I had to take seriously, as something beyond any rational explanation. The odds of picking up an article about Joe DuMais on one of the inside pages of the New York Times in Madison, Wisconsin, after a great deal of thought, were, conservatively, millions to one. "This is much more than a *coincidence*," I declared to myself. An uneasy feeling of trying to cope with the supernatural, the unknown gripped me, and to this day, I feel the same dread and expectation of another such *coincidence* linking me to Joe DuMais. I'm glad I resisted the impulse to walk up to that old man on Market Street. Who knows? It could have been one more of those so-called *coincidences*.

~~~

47.

Thirty-Two Minutes With William Henry Pratt

In 1962 I had a memorable meeting with a world-famous stage and screen actor, William Henry Pratt. William Henry who, you may ask? Well, of course, he was better known as Boris Karloff.

It was during a three-week run of a play called On Borrowed Time that I got a call from the Old Wharf Theatre and Opera House on lower Alvarado Street in Monterey. Back in those pre-urban renewal days lower Alvarado Street still retained much of the atmosphere of a Steinbeck novel. The theatre wanted some publicity photos of the play's leading actor, Boris Karloff, and I was thrilled to have been called.

Upon arrival at the theatre I was dismayed to find that a stage-hand in charge of the stage lighting had not shown up. I had looked forward to photographing Karloff under actual stage lighting to retain that theatrical, dramatic "feel," but that was not to be. I was standing in the small lobby, looking sour when Karloff and his agent arrived. As I shook hands with him, I nervously blurted out something to the effect of what an honor it was to meet him. He was tall, tanned, and looked very trim for a man in his seventies. What impressed me most was his naturalness and warmth, lack of pretense and inner tranquility. He made all around him feel relaxed and calm.

He seemed to sense my disappointment about not being able to use the stage lighting. He said, "look here, do you have any lights with you? Why not take the photographs right here in the foyer? If you need help setting up, just ask."

As I was rushing around setting up my light stands, camera and tripod, I was thinking about just how I should have the great actor pose for the best effect. My pondering was interrupted by his agent: "You have thirty minutes, Mr. Livingstone; remember, just thirty minutes."

Karloff, amused at my increasingly frantic attempts to set up my equipment, smiled broadly and winked at me, as if to say, "Pay no attention to him. Easy does it."

Once everything was in place, I aimed my key light at an angle that would emphasize Karloff's craggy features. I was just about to ask him to turn his face "just a little to the right" when, needing no direction from me, he turned his face to just the proper angle. He must have been so accustomed to posing under studio lights, he could "feel" whether or not the lighting was right.

During the photography session, I ventured to ask him some questions. "Mr. Karloff, which do you prefer, the stage or films?"

Without a moment's hesitation he replied, "By all means, the stage. Nothing compares with the satisfaction one feels when on sees, hears, and senses the audience, right there out in front, responding to the performance. Now as for films, your only audience consists of a director, and he is quite often looking for and finding flaws in you performance. Then too, much of what you thought was your best work ends up on the cutting room floor. The play's the thing."

His gentle, patient way of responding emboldened me to make a personal comment: "Your name sounds very Russian, yet you seem so very English."

Again a big smile. "Oh, that's my professional name. I was born William Henry Pratt. Now, that's no name for an actor, is it? I resurrected the name Karloff from one of my mother's distant ancestors, and just picked out of the air, so to speak, my Christian name, Boris. So there you have it: Boris Karloff."

"The part of Dr. Frankenstein's monster, a part you made famous, did you enjoy that particular part?"

His eyes closed and the furrows in his brow deepened. He was deep in thought before answering: "Those Frankenstein films were a great challenge, and were most difficult for me. More vexing and difficult than the daily three to four hours it took for makeup and for building up my spare frame to acquire a monster's proportions, apart from all that, there was the need to be continually feeling the pathetic aspect of being a physical monster, yet possessing human sensibilities, even a sense of dignity. To this day I still wonder if I had played the part as well as I should have."

I looked at my watch. The time had flown by. It was already two minutes past the time allotted to me. Karloff's agent came in and announced, "Time's up, gentlemen." He reminded me of pub owners during my pub visits in the U.K. in 1944.

Karloff again winked at me and said, "I hope I didn't break your camera with this face of mine." As a professional photographer I had heard this self-effacing quip many times before, and I had a stock answer: "Oh, no, don't worry. It's a heavy-duty camera." But somehow that reply didn't seem appropriate.

~~~

48.

At The Risk of Being Misunderstood

"Don't you hate name-droppers?" I had once asked my wife. "You mustn't hate anyone," Nancy countered. "Why don't you just say that you don't understand them, and let it go at that?"

After a long period of soul searching, I'm going to take the risk of being *misunderstood* as a name-dropper, just this once. Any lingering misgivings I'm casting aside, to share a few anecdotes culled from my friendship of more than thirty years with no less personage than Kim Novak.

Down through the years as a professional photographer I have met many actors and actresses. Among them are two local residents who had achieved the appellation of, for want of a better term, "movie star." Both of them on the occasions I photographed them - impressed me as aloof, cold, feisty bundles of neuroses. Their names shall remain undropped.

What about Kim Novak? You may well ask. I would describe her as a quiet, thoughtful, poetic soul. A lady of high artistic achievements not only on the silver screen but on the artist's canvas as well.

In contrast to the two non-aforenamed local actresses, when I met Kim Novak there was no limp handshake, no averted eyes, no chilly condescension. Instead, I found a sincere, articulate, unassuming, beautiful lady with a smile that was totally disarming. I've asked myself many self many times: Could this be the same Kim Novak reported to have tamed such tyrannical movie moguls as Harry Cohn and the highly abrasive director, Henry Hathaway? I still wonder to this day if there aren't actually *two* Kim Novaks.

In 1963 Kim had fallen in love with and purchased a small castle-like house set on a rocky promontory on the seashore a few miles south of Carmel. Through her large picture windows the restless Pacific Ocean made itself noticed and heard, day and night. Kim confided that although it was the closeness to the sea that attracted her to the house, during stormy winter nights in order to get some sleep she would have to take refuge at the nearby Highlands Inn.

I recalled some years before, having met Pulitzer prize-winning playwright Martin Flavin, and photographing his large, English-style home next to Kim's. Flavin showed me his study in which he had effectively blocked any view of the sea by installing colored leaded bottle glass windows so that he could concentrate on his writing.

One morning while I was visiting Kim at her home, she was having her painting contractor finish applying a coat of cranberry-red paint to the walls of her bedroom. The soft, yet assertive color had a tranquilizing effect I never would have thought possible, and it set off beautifully her yellow brass bed which stood on a thick, solid white rug. She had just turned on a lively Souza march on her record player, which left no doubt in my mind that she wanted the painters to move faster. It was then that I met for the first time her Great Dane, Warlock, who was far more aloof and indifferent to visitors than his famous owner.

On one occasion Kim introduced me to her mother, Blanche Novak, who was visiting her. I took several pictures of mother and daughter with the house in the background.

Kim later told me that the first time her mother approached the front entrance, her mother, having to walk on a short catwalk-like footbridge in order to reach the front door, panicked when she looked down at the churning water below on both sides, holding on for dear life to the two cables that served as handrails.

One evening, my wife's parents, my wife and I hosted Kim and her school days chum and assistant Barbara Mellon at our home for dinner. Kim shared with us amusing anecdotes about her recent visit to the Soviet Union. Upon arrival in Moscow, she and Barbara checked in at the American Embassy and were briefed on what to expect. They were told that in all likelihood their hotel rooms would be "bugged," and their conversations recorded. They were advised to speak only in whispers, and to play the radio loudly in order not to be overheard. By the time they left the USSR and arrived for a skiing holiday in Austria, so habituated had they become to whispering to each other, they caught themselves whispering every time they went to their hotel rooms.

Kim related how, during a banquet given for her by Soviet film industry officials, she sought to "liven up" the proceedings that evening by pointing to a large portrait of Lenin looming on the wall over her, and asking her hosts, "Who's that?" When her question had been interpreted into Russian, her humorless hosts sat in horrified silence.

Chicken à la Chagrin

During our dinner party, while attempting to cut my roast chicken into more manageable morsels, my knife slipped and sent half my chicken portion careening across the table, barely missing landing in our distinguished guest's lap. I sensed the embarrassment and vexation of my in-laws; I had definitely fallen from grace due to my clumsiness. But Kim's reassuring smile and what I mentally felt to be a wink shielded me from the feeling of embarrassment and chagrin that I had every reason to feel otherwise. A few weeks later, during the month of August, my wife, three daughters and in-laws rented a cottage at Lake Tahoe. Since August was one of my busiest months, I was obliged to stay and work in Carmel. One morning Barbara Mellon called me and asked if I was free to accompany Kim, Barbara and Barbara's boyfriend to the Monterey County Fair's Horse Show. It was an invitation I avidly accepted.

Kim is one of those individuals who feels a love and kinship with animals, and high among her favorites are horses. All during the lengthy horse show Kim's attention was riveted on the beautiful animals being put through their paces in the arena below us. Ever mindful of the attention her presence would attract from the crowd, she had artfully disguised herself with a wig, a scarf, and dark glasses. Even so, a few recognized her, but she didn't allow it to spoil her enjoyment of the show.

Kim kept her own horse at a stable out in Carmel Valley, and allowed my young daughters to groom and ride her horse on many occasions

Speaking of using disguises, Kim had asked me to photograph the wedding of her business manager's daughter at Highlands Inn. Norma Kassel, her manager was another long-time friend whom she had met in Chicago years before she became an actress. Not wishing to draw attention away from the bride, Kim arrived at the wedding so well wigged and so inconspicuously dressed, that even when she was recognized, all present sensed and respected her deep desire for anonymity, and admired her for it.

For many years I had submitted black-and-white exhibition prints to the Monterey County Fair. During the year 1964, I felt uncertain about what to pick for that year's competition. I couldn't make up my mind on which print to submit. An accomplished, trained sketcher and painter, Kim has a wonderful pen and ink head of Christ, which she had reproduced on Christmas cards one year and she had shown me a portrait of her mother in oils, which was tender and heart rending. Once she had told me, that while she was in a hospital in New York City recovering from hepatitis, she was painting a portrait of her friend Aly khan's favorite horse when word came that Aly Khan had been killed in an auto accident. She copied Aly's eyes from a photograph and painted them into his horse's portrait.

I asked her to decide for me which of several prints she thought had the best chance of winning. Without hesitation she picked one which I thought had the least chance of all. It was a photograph of a cluster of rusting barbed wire against a cloudy, moody sky. I went along with her suggestion. The photo Kim recommended won the blue ribbon that year. As a token of my appreciation, I split the blue ribbon down the middle and gave one-half to her. A few months later, during a trip to Brazil, Kim sent me a hand-carved ebony good luck charm.

During the summer of 1976, I was taking photos of the two-hundredth anniversary of the founding of San Antonio Mission in South Monterey County. A barbecue followed a colorful reenactment of the arrival at the site of some fifty Spaniards mounted on magnificent horses. As a line formed for the barbecue, I felt a tap on my shoulder. It was Kim and

Salinas veterinarian, Dr. Bob Malloy, whom she had married just a few months before. They both obviously were very happy and devoted to each other. I liked Bob the first minute I met him. He was just as down-to-earth and unassuming as Kim. Kim had chosen well.

These days, Kim and her husband spend a lot of their time on their ranch in Oregon, where they raise llamas. The exciting, tempestuous years of "stardom," of Kim's life in the 'sixties must now seem to her to have been in another incarnation.

So there you have it. I have become a "name-dropper" of the worst kind, but it was out of a spirit of sharing memories of a lovely lady. I hope you haven't *misunderstood* me.

~~~

49.
Waiting for Elizabeth

One November afternoon in 1964 I received an invitation I couldn't turn down. Two nationally known Carmel sculptors, Malcolm Moran and Donald Buby asked me to accompany them down to Big Sur to meet and photograph Elizabeth Taylor and Richard Burton. My friends had completed a bronze sculpture depicting sandpipers over a jade rock, symbolic of Mr. and Mrs. Burton's soon to be completed film, *The Sandpipers*. They asked me to take photos of their presentation of their work of art to the Burtons.

The Sandpipers, it turned out, was the story of a married headmaster of a private boys' school who had a calamitous affair with a beautiful "hippie" painter who lived in a rustic "pad" on a cliff overlooking the Pacific.

Looking back on that film, the critics had a field day deriding and panning the story, in spite of which, (or perhaps because of which) the film became a box office hit. So much for the power of cinematic critics.

We arrived at the site precisely on time, at seven p.m., and were directed to a gleaming aluminum trailer-caravan, the Burtons' dressing-room. Through the open door we saw Richard Burton seated at a low table, puffing on a cigarette, reading a little red book. He stood up to greet us with an engaging smile. I was surprised to see that he wasn't much taller than my five feet seven inches.

He was wearing a shirt with rolled-up sleeves with a loosely knotted knit necktie hanging over his shirt's open neck. What struck me most was his thin, unmuscular arms, so out of accord with a barrel-shaped chest. His deep facial acne scars were somewhat softened by thick makeup.

He waved us in and announced, "I'm sure you'll be a bit disappointed, gents, but Elizabeth hasn't as yet returned from dinner with friends at Gallatin's in Monterey. Gallatin's, you know, half-way between the hospital and jail, fine location."

Burton had us join him around the table and pointed to the little red book, saying, "I've just read the most delightful work by you local poet, Eric Barker. He's a Welshman through and through. No one sings as feelingly as a Welshman, which of course, you already know."

We were immediately won over by our host when he opened a fresh bottle of wine and poured us each a glass, while he lit another cigarette, and urged us to do the same. Being the only nonsmoker in that little trailer, I wondered if I could stand waiting for Elizabeth. I stationed myself at the open doorway, hoping to gasp some fresh air every few minutes.

From the moment we entered the trailer, he had us spellbound. Witty and loquacious, he entertained us nonstop for over an hour with humorous anecdotes, all of which were too scatological to recall in print. He mentioned that his adolescent years were spent in Swansea, and I told him about being stationed near Cardiff in Wales just after the war in Europe, and had visited Swansea, or what was left of it; the whole center of the city bombed down to the ground. Burton grinned and said, "Do you have any idea what I was doing as a fifteen-year-old during the Blitz? During the air raids, my pal and I would take advantage of the blackout and the noise to make the rounds of telephone call boxes, breaking into the coin boxes and fetching home pockets full of schillings."

243

Burton seemed unabashedly proud of his fearless, picaresque exploits. He went on to describe his meeting Elizabeth and his fascination with her..."despite her shortness of limb." And he added, "Can you imagine this? A senator stood up in the Congress of the United States and proposed that I be deported as an undesirable alien just because I loved to – well, owing to my peccadillos with Elizabeth. Fancy that!"

I looked at my watch. It was almost nine o'clock, and still no Elizabeth. But the time was passing swiftly, and Burton and my two friends, having put the finishing touches to their third bottle of wine, (I was driving, and abstained), the conversation grew looser and louder. One of my friends excused himself and asked Burton where the bathroom was, and Burton's valet, a big, muscle-bound black man, escorted him to the door. When my friend emerged from the bathroom, I noticed him stuffing something into his jacket pocket. The valet noticed it, too and grabbed my friend by the nape of the neck, ordering him to "Put that back where you found it!" The item involved turned out to be a brassière.

Unperturbed by the ruckus, Burton now treated us to a by-rote recitation of one of Eric Barker's poems he had just been reading:

"I lose faith in words in this Big Sur country.
Better to leave unsaid
The poems that cannot describe the highest arcs
Of turning and turning hawks, the mountainous
Voyaging leisure of animal-changing clouds.
What words released from this granite shoulder
Can return like a cliff-falling gull
Translating a mood from the Sea?..."

Waiting for Elizabeth

What was so amazing was that as soon as Elizabeth was to return from Monterey, she and Burton were scheduled to do an important night scene. The entire crew was standing by patiently waiting for Elizabeth so that they could shoot the scene and get to bed. And there sat Burton, completely relaxed, enjoying his wine, his cigarettes and admiring little audience. One would have thought he would be a bundle of nerves, busily reviewing his part in the script, impatient to get rid of us as quickly as possible, but instead, he had just memorized a poem he had just read, and was playing the genial, gracious host.

The trailer-caravan by now was filled with smoke, which floated out the door into the cold night sky. As if by a magician's wand, out of the smoke and into the trailer clambered a tiny, bejeweled Elizabeth, not the least perturbed at her tardiness. After her easygoing husband quipped, "Good morning, my love," we were all introduced to her.

The film's director, Vincent Minelli poked his head into the doorway. "Will Miss Taylor kindly at her earliest convenience join us all on the set?" His voice was tinged with sarcasm.

"Give me a couple of minutes, Vinnie, while I change and freshen up." She said, as she disappeared into the bathroom.

Burton winked at us and proclaimed, "That's my Liz. That's my woman - high explosives in a little package."

Ten years later, Nancy and I were in Portofino on the Italian Riviera. We noticed a big crowd of gawkers peering into a little boutique shop window at the water's edge. It was Elizabeth Taylor and Richard Burton inside! I wondered out loud if Burton would remember me (after all, we had hit it off very well, ten years before, especially when we

245

discovered we were both born on November 10, 1925). We decided to wait for them to come out, and say hello. Five, ten, then fifteen minutes passed, and they were still browsing in the shop. Nancy tugged at my arm. "We have a train to catch!"

This time I didn't wait for Elizabeth.

~~~

50.

Pompidou Center Revisited 1980 & 2001

Then there's always Centre Pompidou, so easy to disparage, so hard to forget, try as you may. It's a statement to the world by a defiant Paris: "Look! I'm here with all my guts and innards showing on the outside, a lesson for you in architectural and structural anatomy. If you don't like what you see, *Tant pis; tant mieux!*" (So much the worse, so much the better!).

The first time I experienced that grotesque expression of rebellion against classical forms was on a visit to Paris in 1980. Named after a recently deceased former President of France, Pompidou Center's pipes and ducts and braces were still freshly painted in primary colors, as if according to some color coding scheme. It looked then new and terrible. Now, after the passage of some twenty years, the colorful veins and arteries of the building were subdued by a patina of dust and soot, pungently reminiscent of a gas works or oil refinery in an industrial suburb.

The Center's broad concrete plaza on a cold January morning in the year 2001 was peopled by a handful of shivering, crouching Chinese scribes displaying placards in English: "Your name in Chinese - 5F/10F." I assume the first quotation was for a first name only. Now, one need not travel all the way to Shanghai to savor this touristic amenity.

On a warm summer day back in 1980 that same plaza was crowded with exhibitionists of every kind: fire-eaters, sword swallowers, "stoned" hippies, and knots of tourists, rubbing their eyes in disbelief at a weird panoply of humanity against the pseudo-mechanistic backdrop of the building.

Today the Center projects a tired, prematurely-aged leftover from some world's fair. Time has not been kind to this scar, this aberration, this visual fiasco. It seems as if it had been conceived and born into this world, predestined for an early demise, first by verbal hatchetry such as mine, and ultimately, and mercifully soon, by the wrecker's ball.

~~~

51.

The Last Time I Saw Paris - January 2001

In the Paris of 1945 the furthest thing in my mind as I took part in rounding up G.I. deserters was to visit my old haunts more than fifty years later. But there I was, in January, 2001, casually mentioning to anyone who might be interested, that I had been there as a young soldier 'way back in 1945. I was to discover that today's "yuppie" generation had a hard time imagining how anyone from that bygone era could possibly be breathing, talking and walking without hobbling with a cane and sipping Geritol.

As one *patron* (owner) of a Brasserie-Café on the rue de Villiers put it so kindly, *"Mais, monsieur, vous etes vraiment un très jeune ancien!"* ("But sir, you're truly a very young old guy!"). When it came up that Nancy and I were from California, his face lit up and he exclaimed, "I have been there! I tried your wonderful California wines in the Valley of Napa and of Carmel!"

Thinking that anyone from Carmel must be a connoisseur of fine wines (how wrong he was!), he opened up a bottle of champagne and announced, "Now you must share with us this bottle of excellent champagne from my home town in the Champagne region!"

Having just finished a meager continental breakfast and unaccustomed to drinking anything stronger than herb tea, and it being only 9:00 a.m., I would have preferred to postpone the ceremony until much later in the day. But we sensed his resoluteness, and not wishing to offend, we capitulated good-naturedly. Having vivid recent memories of a bitey, sweet gulp of California champagne only this past New Year's Eve, I took a tiny, tentative sip, dreading its bite and cloying, sweet "finish," as the experts put it. This champagne, however, was truly worthy of its name. One needn't be an expert to appreciate its refreshing, dry smoothness and its unassertive, fruity "finish." I so enjoyed it that I had to fight an impulse to drink it as if it were a delicious brew of iced tea on a hot summer day.

"I never thought that champagne could taste this good!" I exclaimed. As a token of my appreciation I took a photo of M. Sabouret, his wife, son and mother standing behind their typical Parisian bar and promised to send them copies.

Our hotel for the first night in Paris was just a block from our new friends' Brasserie, on the Boulevard Berthier. The Hotel de Banville, once a stylish 1930's townhouse, was now somewhat overrated as a four-star hotel. Now I'm being guilty of committing what I have gleefully derided for years, Americans' habit of raving or complaining about the hotels they have stayed in during their visits to the great cities of Europe and the Orient, as if there were nothing else to report. But there were some memorable features about this hotel which must not go unmentioned. First and foremost, was its German-made elevator, made by the Schindler Company in Germany, which wended its way from our sixth floor down to the lobby so slowly, I could have read several chapters of *War and Peace* on the way down. It seems fitting that Hollywood should make a movie about it, and call it "Schindler's Lift."

When I asked the concièrge if there's a view of the Eiffel Tower from our room, she gave a Gallic shrug, and softly intoned, "A little one."

The Last Time I Saw Paris - January 2001

On our tiptoes we could just make out the very tip of the tower's topmost television mast. But the room was large, airy, bright and furnished in charming Provençal style. Discovering in a guidebook that we could get better value at the Hotel d'Angleterre in the fashionable St. Germain des Prés district on the left bank, we moved there the next day.

We took a harrowing taxi ride across Paris to the rue Jacob, where we alighted, quite shaken, from a series of near-misses presided over by our Senegalese driver. As she left us in front of the d'Angleterre, I told her in French, "You really must someday enter you cab at Laguna Seca." She gave me a bewildered look, and thanked me anyway.

The Paris we were visiting was a somber, no-nonsense January workaday Paris, crowded with taxis, cars, buses and pedestrians trying to reach their destinations as quickly and therefore as unsafely as possible. Store windows were full of "Solde" signs, January there as here being a peak time for after-Christmas sales. We did our gift shopping at one of the city's largest department stores, the Samaritaine, and found that despite the favorable exchange rate with our dollar, the prices were still hefty in comparison to prices back home. In a bakery near our hotel when I saw a price tag on one individually wrapped small chocolate chip cookie marked at 10 francs ($1.50) I had a feeling that Paris has seen better economic times.

All in all, the Paris of January, 2001 still has much to offer to first-time tourists, but for repeaters, it's much more its charming self in the spring and summer months.

~~~

52.
A Pebble for Gertrude Stein -2001

During a 1943 university summer semester my American Literature class had briefly exposed me to a few pieces of Gertrude Stein's literary output. Her careless writing style, with its long run-on sentences devoid of any meaningful punctuation, her apparent disdain for the traditional rules of English syntax bewildered and appalled me. Was it the lack of sophistication of a seventeen-year-old from Oshkosh? Could it be that Miss Stein had forgotten more about the craft of writing than I would ever know? What was the secret of her world acclaim?

Anyhow, there were for me more pressing matters to deal with, a second world war raging at the time, and my eighteenth birthday approaching. Determined to avoid the risk, at any cost, of being drafted into the Navy, I enlisted in the Army, to be beautifully trained to break things and kill people.

At war's end in Europe, my artillery unit was pulled out of Czechoslovakia and disbanded. Thanks to my knowledge of French, however rudimentary at the time, I was sent to Paris as a replacement for an Army criminal investigations agent who was shot by a deserter during a raid on a brothel. So it came to pass that night after night I took part in sweeps, hunting deserters, AWOL's and black marketeers.

A Pebble for Gertrude Stein - 2001

Word got out that a famous American author, Gertrude Stein, had returned to her home of some forty years in the rue Christine, having escaped the German occupation of Paris by reaching unoccupied Vichy, France. I had heard from a fellow soldier that she was receiving G.I.'s at nightly soirées in the old European salon tradition. Meeting the *grande dame de lettres* would be a once-in-a-lifetime opportunity for me, an extremely callow, impulsive twenty-year-old, to confront the cold-blooded violator of the rules of English syntax, punctuation and spelling face to face, and to ask her to repent her crimes. Fortunately for Miss Stein, my nightly forays into the Paris netherworld in search of deserters and other G.I. miscreants left me no time to make any such punitive literary pilgrimage to the rue Christine. It's something I have always regretted. Time and encroaching wisdom have by now made me thankful that our meeting never took place. Still, there has always been a nagging regret that we never met.

On a cold, foggy morning during a recent visit to Paris, I decided to visit the long-departed Miss Stein at Paris's dank, sprawling Père Lachaise Cemetery. I went to the cemetery office to ask for the location of Miss Stein's grave-site. A remarkable look-alike of the French actor Gérard Dépardieu handed me a map and pointed to the farthest edge of the map, saying, *"Le voilà, Plot 94."* Even his voice was Dépardieu's! As I trudged up the steep hill on a narrow, roughly cobblestoned road hemmed in by a forest of mouldering family tombs, I wondered, could that famous star of stage, screen and television possibly be moonlighting between films? Was he there researching some famous long-gone Frenchman he was going to portray? In Paris, anything seems possible.

The unfriendly cobblestones, the uphill climb and the cold wind were taking their toll on my spine and feet. I sat down on a moss-covered tombstone; my determination to visit Miss Stein was evaporating rapidly. A cemetery worker driving by took pity on me and invited me to climb aboard and let me off in front of Plot 94. Thanking him profusely, I mentioned that I had been a U.S. soldier in Paris in 1945. He smiled broadly and replied, *"Et moi, je vous remercie de votre 1945."* ("And I thank you for your 1945!")

The first thing I noticed upon arrival at Miss Stein's grave-site was a collection of some twenty small pebbles atop her unpretentious marble tombstone, and at its base a withered, long-stemmed red rose. As a sort of karmic retribution for Miss Stein's occasional disregard for spelling, the tombstone carver, who had carved her birthplace, date of birth and death, had outrageously misspelled her birthplace. Instead of Allegheny, Pennsylvania, he spelled her hometown "Alefghany," for all eternity to see. This was done, of course, in 1946, b.c. (before computers), so he had no recourse to "spell-check."

I placed a pebble among the others, took one last look at the dead rose, and limped back down the road, back to Paris and the living.

After all is said and done, a rose is a rose is a rose, I suppose.

~~~

53.
I Can Go Home Again (Hopefully)

Thomas Wolf once wrote, *"You can't go home again."* Of course, in his case, he was absolutely right. After publication of his monumental *Look Homeward, Angel*, if he had returned to his hometown of Asheville, North Carolina, he would have been ridden out of town on a rail, or worse.

Now, as for my hometown, I hope my candor about my depression-wracked town has not merited the ire of my fellow Oshkoshers. In this final chapter I hope to atone for any negative nuances that may have accrued about my childhood and adolescent years in that "Fair White City on the Winnebago Sea," by stressing the more positive, endearing memories I have of my hometown.

First and foremost, the hard times we lived through during the 1930's fostered a close, supportive and sincere neighborliness, which calls to mind our neighbors, the Kopitski family. Fred, the head of the family, owned a tavern down on Main Street. Fred and his son, Fred Jr. shared a wonderful hobby in their garage: turning beautiful wooden table legs on a small lathe. As a youngster I was impressed with the long hours they devoted to turning a long, square piece of oak into a leg any table would be proud of. Mrs. Kopitski, a wonderful cook, taught my mother and our maid Laura to make *apfel strudel*, commandeering our big dining room table to spread out the long rolls of dough filled with apple slices, raisins and walnuts, dusted with powdered sugar, and left there overnight to "age." At our family's once-a-year canning time, she would come over and lend her expertise putting up strawberry, peach and grape jams into our vast collection of Mason jars. Our cellar was turned into a cornucopia, with shelves full of carefully labelled jars sealed with paraffin. At Christmas time, the Salvation Army could always count on a bountiful donation of canned jams from our cellar.

Then of course, I've already mentioned earlier the camaraderie my father enjoyed with Chief of Police Gabbert, officers Copey Hansen and MacDonald, and with our town Mayor, His Honor, George Oaks, all of whom conspired once each year to turn our cellar into a winery. All during the winter months our family stoically put up with the rather daunting aroma of fermenting grapes wafting up from the basement.

My mother annually showed her respect and appreciation for my teachers by hosting a dinner/bridge/ma jong party, awarding bottles of our cellar's latest vintage to appreciative (at least outwardly) prize winners.

As a youngster growing up in Oshkosh, I made a few good, lasting friends. Stanley Anderson, son of a fundamentalist preacher, and Richard Otto, son of an Episcopal vicar, I've mentioned earlier. When I was twelve, my closest friend, Gerald Tannenbaum, moved to Milwaukee, and asked me to write to him. Being brutally frank and insensitive at that age, I said, "No, I hate writing letters." I'll always remember the hurt look on Gerald's face on hearing this. Needless to say, I never heard from him again.

I still correspond sporadically with my old friend Dick Hetzel, now a retired architect and businessman living in Kansas City. At the age of fifteen, Dick's six-plus foot altitude towered over me, and his big feet, size fifteen, earned him the nickname "Platterfoot," which he always used when signing his homework and test papers. He was, even in his early teens, an expert fly tie-er and fly fisherman, and still enters national competitions. The only other fly tie-er I have ever heard of was the CIA's famous Director of Internal Security, James Jesus Angleton, who was eventually prevailed upon to retire after having become phobic (perhaps justifiably) about "moles" infesting the CIA.

Another friend, Vance Leuthold, when we were about sixteen, somehow prevailed upon me, a devout non-swimmer, to share in the cost of having a diving helmet built from an old discarded hot water heater tank. We would be able to explore the bottom of the mighty Fox River, he promised. We took our tank to a welding shop operated by a little, good-natured mechanic, Mr. Dietz. He enthusiastically gave hours of his time and skills for a mere two dollars. When it seemed we should have a window to see out of the helmet, Mr. Dietz found an old brass garden hose ring, and fitted it exactly into a circular hole he had cut in the side of the water tank.

He cut shoulder-shaped notches on each side of the tank and lined the sharp edges with lengths of soft rubber garden hose to protect our shoulders. Then he cut a circular piece of glass and cemented it into the hose ring. We were mightily impressed with his craftsmanship, and offered to pay him an additional fifty cents, which he declined to accept. Once the helmet was completed, he announced, "Well, boys, before you go diving in this thing you really ought to buy about fifty feet of rubber hose and an air compressor. Without the air compressor, you'll be inhaling river water by the gallon."

At this point, we regretfully abandoned our project for less expensive, less hazardous activities. In a recent 'phone call to Vance, who is a retired colonel and bank executive living in Nevada, I was touched to hear that he still displays our helmet on his garage wall.

My old friend and mentor, Art Kannenberg, long since passed on, was curator of our City of Oshkosh Public Museum. I may have mentioned him earlier as the man who let me borrow a half-dozen Spanish carbines captured in the Spanish American War, for me to use in training my Cub Scouts in military drill, for which I was ousted from the Boy Scouts of America. When I returned home from the war in Europe, I donated to his War Room a Russian Helmet I had found in a bombed-out SS barracks at Berchtesgaden, a Hitler youth dagger (at least one in every German house), a Nazi arm band and a swastika flag (both as plentiful in Germany as lake flies on a hot summer night under an Oshkosh street light). That flag I had used to line my sleeping bag during cold nights in the boondocks of Bavaria.

Oshkosh, I'm told, has grown considerably since I left for the last time in 1950, and without even seeing my hometown, I feel certain that its growth has been controlled in an orderly, esthetically pleasing way, a tribute to a well-ordered community of prudent, hard-working people. Our Main Street today may no longer resemble the Main Street portrayed by Sinclair Lewis.

I can go home again to Oshkosh, and I look forward to it more than the written word can express.

~~~

Index

About the Author

Photojournalist/columnist/World War II veteran/Cold War intelligence officer John Livingstone recalls his often humorous, at times poignant adventures dating back to the Great Depression years in his hometown, Oshkosh, Wisconsin.

Printed in the United States
19968LVS00001B/85-99

9 781418 455088